Spotlight

on
Technology in the
Music Classroom

Spotlight
on
Technology in the
Music Classroom

MENC The National Association for Music Education

*MENC would like to thank the MEA state editors throughout the country,
who oversee and facilitate the distribution
of essential information to MENC members in their state.*

Production Editor: Elizabeth Pontiff
Assistant Production Editor: Andrea Keating

Contents

Section 4: Technology and Web Resources

Section 5: Computer Technology: Hardware and Software

The *Spotlight* series comprises articles that have appeared in magazines of MENC affiliates over the past several years. The purpose of the series is to broaden the audience for the valuable work that is being done by music educators across the country. Were it not for the dedication of the state editors and article authors, this series would not be possible. MENC would like to thank these individuals for their contributions and to encourage others to share their expertise through MEA and MENC publications.

Introduction

Science has rather abruptly presented us with a brand-new kit of powerful pedagogical tools. ... That we ought to use them is obvious. Not to do so would be an admission that we are capable only of horse-and-buggy planning in an atomic age. But the crucial question is: How, and for what purposes?[1]

The powerful pedagogical tools referred to are radio, television, the phonograph, and the film strip. These words are the opening of a 1947 article in *Music Educators Journal* and are applicable even today. Technology continues to supply an abundance of new pedagogical tools. Any technological tool in the classroom, from a simple CD player to complex composition software, must be thoughtfully integrated into the curriculum. Successful teachers use technology because it contributes to learning, not just because it is available.

Technology can be a teacher's friend or enemy. It has many uses in the classroom—especially the music classroom. Teachers can use it to streamline their administrative tasks, tutor students in ear training, and open new ways for young musicians to compose. But technology is a poor substitute for a well-planned curriculum based on the National Standards. Some see technology as the solution to any problem, whether it is appropriate or not.

The ideas in *Technology in the Music Classroom* range from lists of Web resources to ideas for how to use a single computer with eighty band students. There are hardware and software suggestions as well as recording equipment recommendations. There is also advice for choosing software for the music classroom. Examining why to use technology in the classroom at all is the subject of one of the chapters.

Because this book contains reprints of articles that have previously been published in state journals, and because technology continues to evolve, some of the Web site listings and software packages may no longer be available. That does not mean that the ideas are not still useful. A search on the Internet can usually locate similar resources.

The world is changing quickly and technology along with it. Consider this book a way to get started, and explore some of the possibilities of technology in the music classroom.

Note

1. James L. Mursell, "Audio-Visual Tolls: A Challenge to Educational Vision," *Music Educators Journal,* (33)4: 21 (1947).

Section 1

Teaching with Technology

 Section 1

Teaching with Technology

One Computer and 80 Band Students! Some Technology Applications for Large-Ensemble Classes
Fritz Benz

From MIDI to instant Internet access to software that enables truly innovative teaching strategies, technology offers exciting possibilities in the music classroom. In this article, I hope to share some of the ways we have brought technology into the large ensemble classes in our school.

Teaching band/chorus or orchestra in a large (over 40) class setting presents some challenges for the teacher hoping to infuse technology into the learning environment. At a time when the community and administration are looking for teachers to embrace the technology available in our schools, we are often faced with very large classes that are impossible to bring to the computer lab. If you are fortunate to have dedicated computers in the music area, they may be older models, or you may only have a few, making the realization of a class-size music lab impractical or impossible. While such a lab would be preferable and ideal, we need strategies for dealing with the lack of such equipment and for the larger classes in general.

The Single Workstation Setup
We bring the technology into our classes using a single computer with a large screen 30″ Sony monitor and enhanced sound system. This single unit sits in our band room and is Internet ready, has a connected MIDI tone generator (Yamaha MU5) and has an enhanced sound system attached. For playback purposes, I can connect the computer to the stereo system in the room for even louder playback. In our daily band classes, students enter the room and see the lesson for the day and all relevant announcements displayed on a two-page Microsoft PowerPoint presentation on this monitor. Daily lessons can be created and saved in a file for reference like a planbook and the large screen acts like a video chalkboard but without the chalk dust, white-board markers, or erasers. This entire computer setup is located on a large stand that can be wheeled out to the chorus area or into the band area as needed.

Web Site Display
Internet access in your room is critical. Statewide, many schools are getting wired for such access. We have a single Ethernet connection box dropped into the room with two possible connections. With the Internet access, we can display Web pages on the large screen that relate to a composer or composition. For our fall concert, the band performed one of the Moehlmann transcriptions of a Bach Prelude and Fugue in B-flat. I was easily able to locate a MIDI music library and played the students the piece as it might have originally sounded on the organ. Without access to a vast record or CD collection, this MIDI file was a suitable replacement and listening to it helped us shape an appropriate interpretation of the work.

As the students enter or leave the classroom, they may also view a picture and brief biography of a noted composer of one of our band pieces. Many times this Web page may have a sound clip that I play for them as they enter the room. This exposure in class whets the appetite for further study at the site that students can do at home or in school.

Using Accompaniment Software
During the warm-up phase of class, we sometimes have fun with our circle of fourths scales by playing along with an accompaniment created in Band-in-a-Box. (If you haven't checked this program out, you really should!) A tone generator or synthesizer

should be used as the MIDI sound source, however, a decent soundcard in your computer would also suffice. We have played scale patterns along with a Latin or swing groove, adding some variety to the daily scale performance. The sound is hooked into the stereo system in the room and is loud enough for everyone to play along with.

In jazz ensemble, the soloists on various tunes can be isolated to work on their solos with Band-in-a-Box. Also, any part of a computer-generated jazz combo can be muted to enable rhythm section players to practice comping. Any accompaniment can be dubbed to tape for the student to practice at home, giving every student the opportunity to practice with a rhythm section.

Along with Band-in-a-Box, we have been using SmartMusic (formerly called Vivace) accompaniment software in both choral and band classes. SmartMusic plays an accompaniment to predesignated songs that can be set to actually follow the student's own personal musical interpretation. A small microphone attaches to the shirt or instrument as the student plays. If an accelerando, ritardando, or fermata is performed, the music follows the student! In our middle school band, I break the students into sections to work on small ensemble pieces once a week. During December, they all worked on the same Christmas quartet and played their piece along with SmartMusic. I hooked the microphone on the section leader leading the ensemble and the accompaniment (a full orchestra!) played along! Besides being great fun, it was musically rewarding to the students and gave them the chance to play these unique settings.

Classroom Music Theory Applications

Like many of you, we have several very good music theory programs with ear training components. In our band class, we have been able to do ear training and identification of intervals, chords, etc. with the computer. While this is possible with a simple piano, what the software offers is the visual sight of the staff and/or keyboard as you play.

In middle school band, percussionists are faced with mallet parts more frequently and often do not possess the skills to read notation effectively. Also, when switching students from treble to bass clef instruments, they need the drill work to learn the new clef. I can put a few kids each day on the computer to drill note names, clefs, and basic rhythms while the rest of the band works on something else. I have found this to be very effective in getting our kids caught up to their peers in these areas.

Using E-mail!

In the high school band, I use e-mail to send Web sites, assignments, or other information to the students. I polled the band members at the start of the year and found that about 90 percent of the class had Internet access at home and had or could get an e-mail address. With this capability, it became clear that I could be reaching the students in very different ways.

For those with the capability, I send announcements, reminders, assignment sheets, and Web sites for research, all the while posting this information on the board for those without it. Once you put the e-mail addresses into your address book, it simply becomes a matter of writing the message once and sending it to the group. I sometimes send a personal message to students congratulating them on a great concert or for a great solo. They really appreciate the personal attention! For the students without a computer or Internet access, I might print out the address of the Web page I want them to investigate or post it on the bulletin board. From there they can visit the library or computer lab on their own free period and do the necessary research.

Many teachers have created Web pages of their own for students to visit and go to linked sites on the Web! Both of these strategies offer opportunities for you to utilize this exciting medium for your classes.

Conclusions

Music teachers are some of the most dynamic and creative people on any school faculty (a biased opinion, I know!). Effectively using computer technology in your class is a matter of being resourceful and innovative, especially when you don't have the class size, equipment, or facilities to have an ideal setup. The ideas presented here represent only a small number of possibilities. A fairly modest investment in a newer computer system, large screen monitor, and Ethernet/Internet link can help you and your students explore new and exciting areas of music education. Our use of this technology has helped us demonstrate the need for a dedicated MIDI lab that we are currently putting together in an adjacent room. I hope some of these ideas can be useful for you in your classes!

This article originally appeared in the Winter 1999 issue of the Rhode Island Educators Review. *Reprinted by permission.*

Teaching Music with PowerPoint
James Frankel

Picture yourself teaching general music to sixth graders. It's January, the winter concerts are over, and it's time for a lesson on the music of the American colonial period of music. You are standing at the blackboard writing for the third time that day about penny broadsides when your chalk breaks. The students wake up from their state of semiconsciousness to giggle. You look down in disgust at your chalk-covered hands that are so dry that you could easily light a match with them. The thought enters your mind that it might be time for a career change. "There must be a better way!" Relax. There is.

Let me introduce you to a powerful piece of teaching software that will not only eliminate the use of chalk forever, but will save you time, and money (no more hand lotion), and even make penny broadsides infinitely more interesting to your sixth graders. PowerPoint is part of the Microsoft Office Suite, and most schools have it installed on every computer already. For those of you who are already familiar with PowerPoint after sitting through countless presentations with staff developers who use it, or perhaps even using it yourself, you already know how powerful the software is. For those of you who are not familiar with the software, I strongly urge you to get to know it.

What PowerPoint basically does is allow the user to create a slide show. The user can put anything that they choose on each slide, including text, pictures, narration, sound clips, videos, links to Web sites, animation, you can even draw on each slide just like John Madden. The slide show can be controlled either with a click of the mouse, or it can be set up to run automatically. All of these features combined make PowerPoint an extremely effective teaching tool. While there is little doubt that creating a slide show for each lesson you teach can be very time consuming, in the long run, it is more than worth the effort.

Getting Started
Obviously the first thing you have to decide is what the subject matter of your lesson is. For the purpose of this article, let's stick with penny broadsides from the American colonial period. The first thing that you need to do is gather information that will be included in the slide show. If you have a textbook that you have been using that contains pictures or graphics that you would like to include, you can use a scanner to import the images into the slide show. Another terrific resource is the Internet. Just type "penny broadsides" into a search engine and you'll be amazed at what you'll find. Download as many pictures as you'd like. There are even recordings available of accurate performances of original penny broadsides. Save all of this information onto your hard drive, or just copy and paste directly in to your slide show. Once you have all of your resources gathered, you are ready to create your slide show. When creating slide shows, think of yourself as a film director. You are completely in charge of how the information will be presented to your students.

Open the program; you will be asked whether you would like to create a blank presentation, or use a template. I recommend using a template at first, as it makes the background of each slide a bit more interesting. Next you will be asked to select the format of the slide. Choose the title slide. You will then be shown a blank slide with two text boxes. The one on top is for the main title, and the one underneath is for a subtitle. Simply click on each box to insert text. You can change the text font, size, and style just as if you were using a wordprocessor. The final step you should complete on the title slide is selecting the transition and animation for your slide. To select this option, go to the slide-show pull-down menu and select either slide transition or animation. Experiment with different animations and transitions. Choose one that you like.

The next step is to create your next slide. You can do this simply by going to the file pull down menu and selecting a new slide. Once again, you will be asked to select the format for the new slide. There are a number of options. Choose the one that best fits the sequence of information that you will be presenting. If you would like to insert a picture in this slide, it is quite simple. The easiest way is to select the slide format that has a picture on it. Once you have done that, all you have to do is double click on the picture and the program will ask you from where you would like to get the picture. If you have downloaded a picture off of the Internet, it is as simple as remembering where you saved it. You can also select clip art that comes with the Microsoft Office Suite. Once you have selected the picture it will appear on the slide. All that you have to do is adjust it to the size that you want. Next, add text and your slide is complete. Remember to always add slide transitions and animations, if desired. There are a number of other features such as including video, sound, and narration, all of which are accessible from the insert pull-down menu. One piece of advice however; if you want to play music during the slide show, it is easiest to put a CD into your computer's CD drive and have PowerPoint play the examples from the CD. Using MP3, Real Audio, AIFF and WAV files is also quite simple, but it uses far less memory. Once you save an MP3 into the slide show, it adds to the files overall size quite a bit. As we do not all have computers running at 600 MHz and tons of RAM yet, I highly recommend using CDs. If you have any questions about how to perform any of the functions I have just mentioned, simply use the help menu that PowerPoint provides. It is very thorough and should answer all of your questions.

Once you have mastered the operational functions of PowerPoint, which shouldn't take you very long, you are then only limited by your imagination on how to use it in your classroom. The idea is so simple. Once you have created each slide show, you can permanently save it on your computer and use it year after year. As someone who has been teaching middle school general music for 9 years, I know how difficult it is to get really valuable and age-appropriate resources for middle

school students. Most of the time, I wind up creating the materials myself. Now, using PowerPoint, I can create my own materials that look professional, that are far more interesting than older resources and contain the materials that I want to teach, or that my curriculum wants me to teach.

I strongly recommend that you try using PowerPoint during one of your lessons this year. In order to do so there is one catch. You will need a projection device of some kind. There are inexpensive ways to connect a computer to a television. Ask your school computer person about how or if you can do this in your school. The other option is to use a more expensive projector, preferably one that is bright enough so that you do not have to turn out the lights while you are teaching. If you have either of these means of projecting your PowerPoint presentations to your class, try it.

This article originally appeared in the March 2002 issue of New Jersey's Tempo. *Reprinted by permission.*

Need Some Help in the Classroom?
Diane Gourley

You're strapped for time. You need to rehearse parts to a song, but you know it's going to take more time than you have available to pound out the notes over and over for your students to learn their parts. You wish you could make it happen a lot faster, but you don't know what to do. Does this sound familiar? Well, maybe you need some help in the classroom. This is where a sequencing program can come to the rescue.

A MIDI sequencing program is software that allows you to record individual parts to songs and play them together or separately. A really good sequencing program will let you manipulate individual aspects of the music like tempos and dynamics and also let you set volume levels for each part as well as recording different instrument sounds for individual lines. Sophisticated sequencers can also be used for accompaniments for performances of both groups and individuals; like solo and ensemble festival

My favorite sequencing program is Mark of the Unicorn's (MOTU) Performer. I have been using Performer for about 8 years and it has become one of the best "assistants" I could have in the classroom.

A MIDI sequencer is like a cross between a tape recorder and a player piano: the physical actions you make when playing the keyboard or other MIDI controller instruments are stored not as audio signals (as your tape machine would record) but as numerical information that represents music (pitches, attacks, releases, pitch bends, and more). The nuances in your musical performance are analyzed and its components encoded and stored. When played back, the synthesizer recreates your original performance. In this way, the recorded sequence is more like a player piano roll, telling the instrument exactly how to play itself. One nice thing about MIDI is that you can use any compatible instrument for playback. You can also edit the individual elements of your sequence, such as a single bad note in an otherwise flawless performance. MIDI sequencing provides you with a way to manipulate virtually any parameter of a musical performance.

After I have sequenced a song, I can make tapes for each section with *their* part louder than the others. It is easy for them to hear their part above the harmony of the other parts and they can take the tape to a practice room and practice the song at the correct tempo without having to worry about having someone play it on the piano. This means that each person in the section is responsible for *their* part instead of the poor student who plays keyboard never getting to sing with the other students. It also means that they get a feel for the harmony of the song while they are rehearsing instead of never knowing how their part fits in with the whole.

I can also send a section in to work with the computer instead of the tape and they also have many different options to choose from to accomplish this. They can have their part play louder than the others, they can have it play equal with the others, they can omit their part and just sing it, or they can play only their part omitting all of the other parts. This is particularly useful if an individual student comes in before or after school and wishes to spend time learning a part. It also means *you* don't have to take time out of your busy schedule to "plunk" the notes out for him.

Let me encourage you to investigate the use of a MIDI sequencing program for use with your computer. Performer costs about $285 and my media center bought it for our department instead of purchasing books. Your media center may be able to purchase software programs for your use too. MIDI sequencing is a *very* useful tool that I wouldn't be caught without. It's out there waiting for any use in the classroom that you can dream up. All you have to do is purchase it.

This article was originally published in the Winter 2001 issue of the Arizona Music News. *Reprinted by permission.*

Making the Most of MIDI
Shay Hovell

I find myself spending more and more time with teachers and their students, working to effectively integrate technology and MIDI (Musical Instrument Digital Interface) into traditional music lesson programs. Many smaller Iowa schools have been allotted funds for technology, but teachers are at a loss as to how and where to begin. This article is for those of you who would like to know where to put these monies to make the best use of your school's arts funding.

When I talk to teachers on the subject of MIDI, I stress that there is not a right and wrong way to use the technology. It is rather a means to incorporate more power into their existing music classes. If I walk into an art classroom and present the teacher with the very latest in paints, watercolors, brushes, canvas, and a host of supplies, the art instructor quickly sees how he or she can put these new supplies to use in the classroom. The music classroom teacher should look at the technology offered today with the same feeling of "how can I use these 'supplies' to enhance my existing program?" Listed below are some of the ways music teachers and schools in Iowa are using these new found "supplies."

A fifth grade music instructor(who teaches beginning band students) creates a MIDI file of the music she teaches to beginning students. By first laying down the tracks for all the various instruments and saving a good recording, she begins to teach by having the band play along with the music. Students can hear their parts and learn how the part fits into the master score of the music. As the band rehearses each piece and improves, the teacher weeds out the file altogether. A new trumpeter or saxophonist has the opportunity to hear individual parts played correctly and also to learn what he or she is striving for within a section. This is a great way to get a brand new band playing quickly. And I am sure that in a classroom setting, time is of the essence (to learn music before a concert for Mom, Dad and the whole school). I also know of directors of secondary bands who use this method for the same purpose.

A choral director has basically the same idea as above, but now creates a MIDI file with voices. The accompaniment is recorded onto a track, and all the other tracks are SATB lines. From the first rehearsal, the choir works with the orchestral arrangement of the piece. The instructor increases volume for whatever part the choir is having difficulty singing. Again, the choral lines are deleted as the choir achieves a stronger grip on individual parts. (Note: this is a great way to teach very young children part singing—I have worked with third graders on 2, 3, and 4 part harmonies. For very young choral students, I record the accompaniment and then put instruments of different timbre on each part. I do this so the part is very recognizable to the young ear. An example would be soprano/strings, alto/oboe, tenor/clarinet, and bass/slapbass. When the MIDI file plays all the parts, each pupil is able to hear an individual instrument clearly because of the differing timbres. Once again, as the choir becomes better able to sing parts freely, I can delete these instrument parts so that eventually students are singing with the accompaniment only.)

A junior high band has a student play the MIDI keyboard, simulating an entire string section. The school is too small for a string program, so MIDI has helped to enhance the concert band tremendously. Although the student primarily plays the string sounds, she is also called upon to create any instrument that is lacking in the orchestra.

With current technology it is possible for a full MIDI orchestra to follow a conductor. The old complaint used to be that working with a MIDI file was like singing with a karaoke tape. Those days are gone! Cakewalk in Concert is probably one of the most revolutionary MIDI programs I have seen in my twenty years working with MIDI. With this program I am able to control an entire orchestra in terms of tempo and dynamics just by how I play a keyboard.

Schools are finding Music Ace 1 or 2, a great means of teaching or supplementing a lesson. Many schools use this program for individual computer time, but a few use it as an entire classroom lesson. The teacher is at the main computer and acts as the liaison between the classroom and the program.

Another key ingredient for your MIDI classroom is the keyboard or MIDI device that you will use to input and output your music. This is also a big factor as to how much use your system will get. (Always remember, if it is up to you to purchase these instruments—look to the future. Just because you may not play the piano does not mean that the next teacher likewise will not.) Look for 88, quality, touch-sensitive, weighted keys. I, as a piano player, do not enjoy sitting at a 4 octave non-weighted keyboard and then being expected to perform well.

Huge strides have been made in digital pianos in the last five years . Recently when I was in Vienna, I went to hear a performance by the resident Vienna Chamber Orchestra from the Vienna School of Music. There, in the land of Steinways and Bösendorfers, this amazing group of musicians used a Clavinova Grand Touch as their keyboard of choice for performance. I think that says a lot about the quality of some of these digital pianos.

Technology is now here to stay and will only be getting stronger in all areas of schooling. If you are one of the teachers who knows little or nothing about it, it is time to jump on the MIDI bandwagon. When I see 90-year-old people who are able to send and receive e-mails and use the Internet effectively, there is no reason why we should not be as literate as they. As with anything new, music technology must be learned. I did not learn to drive a car until I sat at the steering wheel—all the driver's education reading and tests only helped to prepare me for the seat behind the wheel. Once in that seat I learned to actually drive. The same is true for the computer—get in the driver's seat and gun that motor.

This article originally appeared in the September 2000 issue of the Iowa Music Educator. *Reprinted by permission.*

Electric and MIDI Stringed Instruments: A Primer for String Teachers
Scott Laird

In an era when technology is constantly changing, many string teachers may find it easier to hold fast to that which is known or comfortable. Yet teachers have a responsibility to their students to be knowledgeable concerning new technology in their field. In the area of string education, that technology includes new variations on stringed instruments. While the use of and the teaching of electric stringed instruments should never replace that of traditional strings, they can be a valuable enhancement to a traditional string program.

Electronic stringed instruments have been available for several years, but recent advancements have made them more complex, more versatile, and potentially confusing to the average string player or teacher. With a little bit of research, however, teachers find that the complexities are easily understood and the technology is not nearly as overwhelming as it appears. In addition, these instruments have many applications in the classroom and the private studio.

Uses in K–12 String Programs
At the elementary level, electric instruments can be a great recruiting tool. They can be demonstrated as something that young students may get the opportunity to use with hard work and practice over the years. Teachers that have used them in recruiting programs boast enthusiastic student response and consistently higher recruiting numbers.

At the middle school level, time with electric and MIDI stringed instruments can be an excellent reward for good work, consistently high practice time, or mastery of a particular technique. At this level, where retention is critical, electric instruments can be a great motivating factor. The MIDI instruments can also be effective tools in helping students feel the correct spacing of fingers as they move to full-size instruments. If fingers are not placed perfectly on the fingerboard, the correct notes will not sound. Electric and MIDI instruments don't mask mistakes, they amplify them. In order for a student to master an electric instrument, he must first master his acoustic instrument. Electric stringed instruments are not a shortcut to good tone quality.

Uses of electric instruments at the high school level are many and varied. First, they may be used to enhance traditional literature. On her spring concert, Kathy Camarata of Centennial High School, Howard County, Maryland, will be featuring senior violinist Dan Buchner as a soloist on the "Ashokan Farewell," with her orchestra accompanying. The Eleanor Roosevelt High School Orchestra in Greenbelt, Maryland, recently performed Vaughan Williams' Concerto Grosso with its electric quartet as soloists and string orchestra accompanying.

Outstanding soloists may use electric stringed instruments with the school jazz band or perform with student rock bands. The climate in popular music today certainly lends itself to the incorporation of electric stringed instruments into the rock and pop format. Many popular groups such as Dave Matthews Band and Smashing Pumpkins are utilizing electric stringed instruments. These possibilities are great for the self-esteem of string students who so often are stereotyped as the serious musicians of the school.

Some strolling string groups use an electric violin as a means of leading the entire group and staying together. In addition, solid-body instruments can be excellent silent practice instruments as they can be played through headphones and not be heard by those around.

These instruments can also be a great tool for beginning improvisation. Mark Sholl, director of orchestras at Hilliard High School in Columbus, Ohio, has been using MIDI instruments to motivate students and to inspire creativity and improvisation for the past two school years.

An electric instrument and a one-second delay can inspire virtually any string player to spontaneous fugal playing. This can be a great first step to improvisation. Students are forced to really listen and anticipate what they want to play next.

Electric Instrument Basics

Electric stringed instruments come in a variety of looks and sound capabilities. A basic understanding of the technology is all that is needed to get started.

Electric violins, violas, cellos, and basses are readily available. Manufacturers range from local luthiers to international companies with worldwide distribution and availability. The technology used in each manufacturer's instruments varies greatly, and every company's instruments sound and feel very different.

These instruments range in shape from a very traditional look to futuristic shapes. Some are hollow, others are solid, and still others have virtually no body at all. Many electric violins are available in four- and five-string models. (The fifth string is a low C string.)

Most electric violas and cellos are four-string models. Basses are available in four-, five-, and even six-string models.

The great majority of electric instruments are analog. Analog instruments send a continuous wave form through an electronic cable from a pickup (which is like a microphone), usually found in the bridge, to the amplifier. Analog electric stringed instruments are much more versatile than most musicians realize and can serve a variety of functions.

As with traditional instruments, each electric instrument is tonally unique and generates a tone that is unlike the instruments of other manufacturers. The key component in an analog electric instrument is the pickup, which sends the musical signal electronically to the amplifier. The pickups produced by different manufacturers are all unique and are designed to serve different purposes. Some pickups are designed to create the most acoustic sound possible. Others are designed to eliminate the chance of feedback—the high pitched squeal associated with acoustic instruments and microphones at stage volumes. Still others are designed to eliminate extraneous bow noise or interference.

String teachers must also realize that the amplifier reproducing the tone plays an important role in the sound of an electric instrument. The size of the speaker, number of speakers, and variety of equalization settings all play an important role in the tone produced. Therefore, priorities are important when choosing an electric instrument. Is the tone most important? The look? The instrument's ability to handle stage volumes without feedback? All of these are factors in making a decision.

MIDI Stringed Instruments

While the analog electric stringed instruments are extremely versatile, MIDI (Musical Instrument Digital Interface) stringed instruments have substantially more applications. MIDI stringed instruments can perform all of the functions of analog instruments. They can be connected directly to an amplifier by a quarter-inch phone plug and utilize all the possibilities of effect processors. They have many additional capabilities as well.

The pitch generated is sent via the pickup system and MIDI cable to a MIDI controller. The MIDI controller is the computer that translates the signal into digital information. The digital signal may then be sent to a synthesizer or a computer, manipulated in a variety of ways, and then sent to the amplifier where the tone is produced. Through this process, the MIDI stringed instrument can produce any of the sampled or pre-recorded sounds that a MIDI synthesizer can produce. It can also interface with any computer program that is able to receive digital musical information, such as notation programs, sequencers, and a variety of other programs.

In using a stringed instrument MIDI system, an entirely new world of musical possibilities opens up to the musician. The instrument can create the sounds of virtually any instrument, from string sounds to woodwind, brass, and even percussion. In addition, the synthesized sounds can be easily combined with the analog sound of the instrument to achieve the life of the analog sound and the ambiance of the synthesized sounds.

Moreover, each string is individually programmable for different sounds. For instance, the E string can be programmed to be a flute, the A string to be a trumpet, the D string a tuba, and so forth.

The MIDI system can be set to read vibrato or to read a glissando if desired. Or, if the player wishes, a glissando on the instrument can sound each individual semitone, as a keyboard would. The system will respond to dynamic variation or can be set to play at only one volume. In addition, notes may be sustained with the footswitch, much like that on a piano. All voices can be transposed up to three octaves up or down from actual pitch. Also, the system permits the player to tune to A 440 Hz, or adjust from 440 Hz to 460 Hz.

The MIDI system can also interface with a standard personal computer. It can be used as an input device for notation programs such a Finale or with sequencing programs that provide the player with a digital multitrack recording opportunity. Virtually any program that uses a synthesizer as an input devise can be used with the MIDI system.

The technology is available. The potential dividends are high. While not a replacement for strong string teaching, pedagogy, and playing; electric and MIDI stringed instruments can be a valuable asset to a string curriculum.

This article is reprinted from the September 2000 issue of the Iowa Music Educator. *It originally appeared in the Summer 1997 issue of the* ASTA Journal. *Reprinted by permission.*

Tips on Music Technology
Karen A. Miyamoto

Today, music teachers are faced with an important decision. Should we make use of the technological advances in the world of music that exists outside of our classrooms? As music educators, many of us feel unprepared to make this decision. The world of music is changing rapidly, and there are so many new options that it is easy to feel overwhelmed and intimidated and ignore the changes.

The prospect of using new equipment need not be frightening. It is important to recognize technology for what it is—simply new equipment. Technological advances need not alter the premises of music education. We are simply dealing with new tools for teaching. In the same way that music does not reside in an instrument, learning does not reside inside computers and technological equipment.

There are basically five types of music software (1) drill and practice, (2) tutorial, (3) music games, (4) composing/printing, and (5) testing software. Each is applicable in different circumstances.

There are many misconceptions about using technology as stated by David Brian Williams and Peter Richard Webster in *Experiencing Music Technology*. Misconceptions may lead to fear and an inability and willingness to learn technology for your classrooms. The top ten misconceptions and some recommendations to alleviate them are as follows:

1. **Technology refers only to hardware.** The decision to purchase a computer or music keyboard is not where the story begins and ends. Hardware is part of a system in which there is much more to be considered.

2. **There is hidden "knowledge" inside the hardware that is intimidating.** This misconception often creates fear in the person using hardware (what some call cyberphobia). Yes, there is a certain amount of knowledge built into a computer by the manufacturer, but only to get things going when you turn it on. Then the machine sits there, dumb and happy, waiting for you, the boss, to tell it what program to run, what data to treat, and what tasks to do.

3. **The hardware might break if something is done incorrectly.** Short of hitting a piece of hardware with a hammer, there is not much you can do to hurt a piece of equipment by using it normally. No computer or music device ever broke because a button was pushed or a key depressed in error.

4. **Computer technology is reserved for the technically elite.** At one time, this was true. However, newer computers and music devices offer much easier to use interfaces between people and the hardware. There are, of course, certain concepts and procedures that need to be understood. And there are times, regardless of our level of understanding, when we must turn to people who are more technically knowledgeable than we are. It is still far easier these days to use technology than at any point in our history. If you have learned to play a musical instrument or sing, you can use a computer or a MIDI keyboard quite effectively.

5. **Computer technology takes too long to learn.** If you are impatient, computers and music technology may not be for you. However, if you have achieved any success in music, it is likely that you have learned how to live with small but important gains from practicing. If you approach computers and music technology in the same way, rich rewards will follow.

6. **Computer technology is only for the young.** Thinking like this is like deciding not to listen to music composed after 1919 or refusing to vote in a presidential election. There is no evidence of biological or psychological attributes in older people that makes them unable to learn to use technology productively. Perhaps this misconception has more to do with open-mindedness and willingness to change than with age and technology themselves.

7. **Using technology removes the creative spirit from music experience, producing music that is antiseptic or sterile.** Sometimes this is true, especially if there is a lack of imagination in the musician responsible or if the tech-

nology does not allow for subtlety. Bad music is bad music! Of course this is true for traditional acoustics as well—a point that seems to be lost on some of technology's harshest critics.

8. **Computers, MIDI, and CD-ROMs, when used for teaching about music, are just another expensive set of technological gimmicks that take time and money away from the real business of music education.** This complicated misconception probably has less to do with technology itself and more to do with beliefs about what teaching strategies and the real business of music education should be.

9. **Technology, not music, becomes the focus.** This can be true when technology is used poorly. If the most interesting aspect of a performance was the performer's ability to play both keyboard and the wind controller while working the mouse on a computer, apparently the music itself did not capture our interest. Musicians who spend inordinate time engaged in the frills of technology perpetuate this misconception. The blame should be placed where it belongs.

10. **Technology replaces musicians jobs.** Yes and no. It is true that certain employment opportunities are affected by music technology, but what often is not considered is the number of new jobs created because of technology and the time saved for more creative work.

Following are some easy tips and lessons using technology in your music class even if all you have is one computer and a television monitor in your classroom. For these lessons, it's recommended that you have a computer with a TV hooked up to it for the class to view. The TV should be high resolution. High resolution units can adequately reproduce the high-quality images of laser videodiscs. The unit should have several inputs for video signals, and if the unit is to be used for audio, it should have quality stereo sound capabilities.

Technology Lesson Plan 1
Grade level: Preschool/kindergarten
National Standard 6: Listening to, analyzing, and describing music

Procedures
1. Go to the Web site address: www.nickjr.com/blue_archive/games/blue106/106_index.tin?weekly=no.
2. The following instruments are included in this game: trumpet, conga drum, guitar, piano, flute, clarinet, and recorder. You may write these words

on a chart or on the board and have students practice saying the names. If you have pictures of the instruments, show them to the students.

3. Introduce students to the musical concept of timbre. Each instrument has a different tone color or timbre which makes it sound different from another instrument or voice.

4. The Web site is a game on listening and instrument sound recognition and identification. It uses the character Blue from the TV show *Blues Clues*.

5. When the game begins, you will see three instruments in the living room. When you hear the sound of one of those instruments, you must click on the instrument that matches the sound. If you choose the correct instrument, you win, and Blue dances to a special musical number.

6. You will hear a different instrument sound each time you play.

7. Have students play the game as a group and then call on individual students to answer.

8. At the end of the session, once again review the names of the instruments.

9. You might have students draw a picture of their favorite instrument.

Technology Lesson Plan 2
Grade Level: 4–6
National Standard 6: Listening to, analyzing, and describing music

Procedures
1. Go to the Web site address: www.nyphilkids.org
2. This is the New York Philharmonic Kidzone!
3. Available on this Web site is the Musician's Lounge (learn about different musicians), Composers' Gallery (learn about different composers), Instrument Storage Room (see pictures of instruments and hear a musical excerpt of the instrument), Instrument Laboratory (construct your own instrument), Conductor/ Soloist Dressing Rooms (learn about various conductors and soloists), and Newsstand Composer's Workshop (learn about various composers).
4. Teach students the four families of the orchestra: strings, woodwind, brass, and percussion.
5. Go to the Instrument Storage Room and show the various instruments and their sounds. Have students categorize each instrument into one of the four instrument families.
6. Explore each of the other categories on the Web site.

Technology Lesson Plan 3
Grade Level: K–6
National Standard 5: Reading and notating music

Procedures
1. Go to the Web site address www.jwpepper .com/demos.html.
2. This page, Pepper Music Network Software Downloads, contains every available demo of the software products that appear in the Pepper Music Technology catalog. You'll also find links at the bottom of the page to the various manufacturer's Web sites. To order any of these software products, log on to the online catalog and choose the option "Browse the Pepper Catalogs." Then select "Software" from the catalogs listed.
3. Experiment playing with these demo downloads. Many of the demo versions are useable except for certain features (such as saving, hall of fame, access to higher levels, etc.).
4. Some good demos to begin with are Clef Notes, Music Flash Cards, and Early Music Skills.

Technology Lesson Plan 4
Use an instant music program such as Band-in-a-Box as a teacher's tool to create accompaniment parts for group rehearsal, individual practice, and improvisation. Suppose you would like to create an accompaniment for a song in general music class, chorus, or an instrumental ensemble. With Band-in-a-Box, it is as easy as typing in the chord symbols and playing the melody. Once the accompaniment parts have been created, it is easy to make a cassette recording for individual students to take home for practice. Simply connect the output of the MIDI keyboard or computer sound module to a cassette deck and make the recording.

Technology Lesson Plan 5
Use a tuning program to help students improve their pitch awareness. Some instrumental and general music class teachers find using a tuning program to be an effective application of computers and technology. The program Tune-It II, published by Electronic Courseware Systems, for the Macintosh, Apple II, and PC, is simple to operate. The objective is to tune two pitches to unison. It offers both visual and aural modes and various levels of difficulty. Teachers can use this program to help students become aware of the tuning process.

Technology Lesson Plan 6

Use a notation software program to:

1. Create études, rhythm exercises, and custom parts for students in band, chorus, or orchestra.

2. Create warm-up exercises. Suppose you have developed some of your favorite warm-up exercises. Notation software can help you to quickly print out these exercises. A notation program works like a word processor. Notes can easily be copied and pasted into other parts of the music. With practice, a notation program will allow you to create professional-looking parts much faster than you could create them by hand.

3. Create ensemble music such as duets, trios, and quartets. As long as the music is original or in the public domain, you can create your own chamber music for any instrument or voice combination.

4. Reduce a piano part so students can accompany a chorus or other ensemble. Many times, the piano accompaniment part is too difficult for student accompanists. Notation software can help the teacher simplify the part.

5. Write your own compositions, arrangements, or even a method book. If you have been avoiding writing original compositions or arrangements because of the cost of having parts copied, notation software remedies this problem. Once the composition has been entered into the computer, you may listen to, edit, and revise it as often as desired.

6. Use the transpose function to quickly print out parts for various instruments. Every good notation program has built-in transposition capabilities. Parts can be entered in concert pitch and then automatically transposed for B-flat instruments, E-flat instruments, etc.

7. Use the play function to play out difficult accompaniments and rhythms. Every notation program has the capability to play out the notes that are entered. If you do not read music well or play the piano very well, simply enter in the notes of the written score and play back the notes to hear what it sounds like. You can enter in the accompaniment for a given score and play it back as background accompaniment for songs, music, etc.

Some recommended basic notation software programs and their (publishers/type of computers) are:

1. Dr. T's Apprentice (Dr. T's/Atari, Amiga)
2. Dr. T's Quickscore Deluxe (Dr. T's/PC DOS, PC Windows)
3. Dr. T's Copyist (Dr. T's/PC DOS, PC Windows)
4. Encore (Passport/Mac, PC Windows)
5. Music Time/Music Time Deluxe (Passport/Mac, PC Windows)
6. Quick Score Deluxe (Dr. T's/PC DOS, PC Windows)
7. Songworks (Ars Nova/Mac)

One of the largest suppliers of software for music education can be accessed at www.lentine.com.

In conclusion, technology is not a cure-all for music teaching, but it can be a useful and resourceful tool that can help to motivate students and teachers as well. Technology can save you many hours of labor if you use it administratively or as an assistant. Learning one new thing at a time can help prevent it from seeming too overwhelming.

This article originally appeared in the April 2000 issue of Hawaii's Leka Nu Hou. *Reprinted by permission.*

Technology Fits
Philip Ponella

In the movie *Dead Poets Society*, Robin Williams plays an English teacher at a traditional, conservative boarding school. On his first day, he asks the students to open the poetry text that had been used for years and asks a student to read the preface aloud. Upon completion of the reading, Williams' character asks all of the students to rip the page out of their books and throw it away. While the tried and true text was the foundation from which poetry was taught at that school for years, it did not fit with his philosophy and method of teaching the subject. He made a powerful statement about the importance of individuality and what it brings to education.

Technology has changed our lives in unimaginable ways. In a short period of time, pointing and clicking has become a part of nearly everything we do. While the new conveniences we enjoy are wonderful, many educators are now struggling to incorporate technology into their teaching. Trying to learn new technologies, many are having "fits," feeling that the very foundation of their tried-and-true teaching methods are being torn out from under them as they work diligently to learn the new skills. While many faculty now use technology, many are doing so merely because of the expectation that they should, not because it improves or enhances the quality of their teaching. It is critical that educators ensure that technology be used as another tool that fits into the curriculum. Most importantly, like Williams in *Dead Poets Society*, it should fit with their personal style, method, and level of comfort.

During my tenure leading technology at the Eastman School of Music, I was fortunate to work with some truly exceptional musicians/educators. The needs of the faculty were complex, and the technological possibilities were endless. Some faculty members, particularly those in the theory and composition departments, had sophisticated technological needs. Others in the performance areas maintained that the primary business of the institution—teaching music—is still best taught by a master teacher working one on one with a student. The technology needed to do this has not changed in well over a hundred years. Most teachers continue to need only an instrument and a music stand (and in some instances a chair!)

So where does technology fit in the curriculum of today's music educator? What skills will students need to have to succeed in a technological future as musicians/educators? As stated above, using technology for technology's sake and without a clear benefit to the teaching and learning process is a mistake. Moreover, personal style and method should dominate how one teaches. We are, however, beginning to see many new uses of technology that have the potential to invigorate the teacher-student interaction.

What can you do right now?

What follow are some suggestions of how technology can be used to enhance the traditional methods of teaching music in the school or university setting.

Learn to use a music notation program

The way word processing has reinvented our writing process, so too has music notation software changed composition, theory, and arranging. Anyone who has ever had to practice from a hastily scribbled exercise on a scrap of their teacher's manuscript paper (or worse, in the back of their book), knows the advantages of seeing something printed off in a clear, neat form. Rather than taking valuable lesson time scribbling, imagine being able to run over to the computer and print out that special left-hand exercise. Or, rather than take the time to do that, tell the student, "I'll e-mail it to you later today."

Many school band/orchestra directors need to re-orchestrate or simplify parts based on the personnel in their groups. This work is done far more efficiently using notation software, where with the click of a mouse, transpositions are quickly done.

Moreover, most notation software will allow you to play back what you have entered. The initial hearing of an arrangement while still at your computer can save countless questions and rewrites after the parts have been distributed.

It is this very feature that can be used so successfully to assist in teaching composition and arranging. Getting students to "hear" what they are writing or to understand the nuances of a small change is a tremendous challenge. With the ability to hear it played back at the computer, the student can produce a much more polished product before ever going to the lesson or rehearsal.

Yes, programs such as Finale and Sibelius can be daunting to learn. However, they are becoming more intuitive. The time invested in learning such a program is time well spent.

Revamp the way you teach ear-training and music theory

Ear training can be drudgery (no offense).

Learning to hear intervallic relationships between tones and identifying chords aurally and visually is difficult. Clearly, this is an area where the more time a student spends practicing, the better they will become. There are numerous software packages that can put a student through a number of drills to better prepare them for the time spent in class. The exercises are progressive and far more interesting than plunking out notes at a piano.

Place the music in context

With the convergence of multimedia technologies, there is a wealth of information available on CD-ROM and the Web that helps students to understand the period from which a piece or composer originated. The importance of understanding the interrelationships between all the arts make music more interesting to the student.

Music minus one for a new millennium

There are products now available that provide computerized accompaniments for standard repertoire with which students can practice. Some commercial products now provide "smart" accompaniment where, by playing into a microphone connected to the computer, the computerized accompaniment will follow the performer as they speed up or slow down. Certainly those of us who grew up practicing with our record players can appreciate the benefit of this!

Commercial products aside, the use of notation and sequencing software allows the same functionality (minus the "smart" accompaniment feature). By entering an accompaniment into the software and playing it back, the student has a built in accompanist with which they can learn the piece. It is, of course, no substitute for a real accompanist with whom one makes music. But the time spent learning a piece is far more productive when intonation and difficult passages can be worked out before sitting down with the accompanist.

The Future

These points, while noteworthy to some, are really just some basics from which to start. We must be mindful of continuing to think about the skills today's students will need to succeed in the future. A recent conversation brought this to light for me. I was meeting with a representative from Apple Computer, discussing the use of technology in the university curriculum. Upon learning of my interest in music, he mentioned something about Harry Connick Jr. and his use of technology (specifically Apple computers). I had not heard anything about this process.

When I returned to my office, I sat down and did a few searches of the World Wide Web. Within a matter of minutes, I discovered an article by Paul de Barros titled "A Chart a Day," published in the October 1999 issue of *Downbeat,* (republished on the Web at www.connick.com). The article describes the bandleader's innovative use of technology. In the article, Connick is quoted saying, "Everyone in the band has flat panel screens and their own computer and monitor on stage, so it eliminates the need for sheet music. They can all make their own edits and dynamic markings and notes."

Later in the article, the author describes Connick working on a new arrangement and a discussion with one of the sax players:

Harry, who has taken dinner alone so he can continue working, walks in with the saxophone parts for "Jitterbug Waltz."

Weldon eyeballs an eight-bar section of 16th-notes. "What's the tempo?"

Harry snaps out a quick pace.

"And we gotta memorize this?"

"Right. 'The Three Tenors.' Up front. You probably want to learn it from the disk though, don't you, rather than putting the paper between you and the music."

"That way I can groove it into my brain."

"You have Finale on your laptop, right?"

"Yeah."

"I'll e-mail it to you."

At the time I first read that, I was planning this article. I thought that I would present a view of the future in which music libraries and musicians would rely increasingly more and more on electronic access to scores and recordings, not unlike the way the rest of us now rely on electronic information in ever increasing ways.

Rather than waste time projecting, I can say with some certainty that the future is here now!

This article originally appeared in the Spring 2000 issue of the Kansas Music Review. *Reprinted by permission.*

What Can I Do with One Computer in My Music Classroom?
Lee Walkup

If your school does not yet have a completely outfitted MIDI music lab with enough workstations to keep 25–30 general music students busy, then this article is for you. The probability is much greater that you just acquired one computer for the music department, and that you share it with at least one or two other teachers. And, you are now wondering how you can use that computer with your band, orchestra, chorus, and general music classes.

First of all, you can be proud that (1) You have entered the wonderful world of music technology, and (2) you are better off with one computer than you were with none.

No matter what level you teach, there are basically eight kinds of software you can use in your music classroom:

- Courseware. This includes informational CD-ROMs, theory drill, music games, or jazz improvisation.
- Sequencing/recording. Sequencing software is used to record and edit music using a MIDI keyboard. There are also many programs that can digitally record live vocals and instruments. And, there are some programs that can do both MIDI and live.
- Algorithmic. This is a fancy word that means that the software can create music by itself (with a little help from the user).
- Music notation. This is software that can help you write and print scores and parts neatly.
- Music utilities. These are special programs for music teachers that can help create music worksheets, marching band drills, etc.
- Record keeping. This is database software that can help the teacher manage lists of students and information about them.
- Text/page layout. This includes word processing software and page layout software that can help create pages with text, art, and pictures.
- Internet browsers. This is free software that will allow you to access the almost limitless information about music that is on the Internet. And, it will allow you to send and receive messages from others electronically (e-mail).

The following are examples of available music software, and their uses, that I hope will be helpful. There are many other titles, but there is not enough space here to include them. Please order the free software catalog mentioned at the end of this article for more information.

Courseware
There are some very good products available that your students can use independently. For learning basic elements of music, Music Ace (CD-ROM, ages 8 to adult) by Harmonic Vision is excellent. There is a sequel, Music Ace 2, that continues where Music Ace leaves off. Each CD has 24 lessons, followed by a game that uses skills taught in each lesson. Sound and graphics are very good and will hold your students' attention. Other titles especially good for students through middle school are Making Music and Rock Rap'N Roll. There are many others.

For students in grades 7–12, there are some excellent theory drill programs such as Practica Musica (Ars Nova), which is now available on both Mac and Windows platforms. This program has been around for a long time, and is an excellent supplement to any music theory course. For Windows only, Auralia is a similar program for independent theory drill. Both of these programs cover intervals, scales, rhythm, pitch, and chord recognition. Alfred's Essentials of Music Theory (CD-ROM, Mac/Windows) was released this past year. Its graphics are very good, and the quality of the instrumental sounds are outstanding! There is one volume out now, with additional volumes scheduled to be released soon. This program has entertainment value, and the content is solid and well-done.

There are some very good historical CD-ROMs available. I can recommend The History of Jazz by Clearvue. Billy Taylor narrates an entertaining historical overview of jazz from traditional through the present. The historical photos and musical examples are good. There are quizzes available for each unit covered.

Sequencing/Recording
You and your students can record music on your computer. There is truly an abundance of sequencer programs available. Some can record using MIDI input only. Some can record MIDI and live instruments. I would suggest that the novice to computer recording learn to record MIDI input first. It is more economical, since it doesn't require any microphones, mixers, or external sound equipment—and it does not require much hard disk space to store. Real digital recording of live sound requires about 5 MB of disk space per minute of music (mono). On the other

hand, using MIDI only, an 8-track, 3-minute piece will probably use no more than 100 KB (150 times less disk space than a digital recording).

Here are three inexpensive, basic, simple-to-use sequencer programs available for both Mac and Windows.

Musicshop (Opcode) is very easy for students to learn. It automatically turns the MIDI tracks into notation right on the screen—and the notation can be printed. Though the rhythm shown on the screen is not always ideal for printing sheet music, it is good enough for young musicians to get a visual idea of what they played. While Musicshop is not primarily meant to be a notation program, students who do not read music will learn some notation concepts just by using it. For the price, it records well and is a snap to learn.

FreeStyle (Mark of the Unicorn) is a very good product that is similar to Musicshop, but is at least a step higher in sophistication. It also has notation. I have heard some good things about this program.

Master Tracks Pro (GVOX) is another excellent choice. It is very inexpensive, and is a rock-solid product. It does not have a notation feature, but is easy-to-learn, logical, and does some things better than Musicshop. Its quantize function (fixing rhythms played out of tempo) is excellent!

For the Windows platform only, the basic sequencer of choice is probably Cakewalk Home Studio (Cakewalk). It is also inexpensive and can record real, live, digital sounds as well as MIDI. (Digital recording works best on a fast computer with a large hard drive.) This product is widely used in many schools and highly recommended.

Algorithmic

You have probably heard of a program called Band-in-a-Box (PG Music). With this program, you can type in the chord changes to a song, choose a style from over 200 available, and play a completed arrangement (with five instruments) in about 2 minutes. For its price, it is an amazing program! It is great for creating background accompaniments for singing. It is equally good for students who are learning to improvise over chord changes. Yes, you can record a melody line of your own over the arrangement. If you want, the program will even create a solo in the style of a famous jazz musician—automatically. And, it will be different every time. This is great for studying styles of playing like Dizzy's bebop, or Coltrane and Miles Davis.

You can record the MIDI output of your keyboard to a cassette deck. You can leave these tapes

for a substitute teacher to use with your class, if the need arises. Your instrumental students will enjoy playing fun tunes, along with a "band." There are endless uses for this program. It is inexpensive and highly recommended.

Notation

There are simple notation programs such as PrintMusic (Coda Music Systems) and MusicTime (GVOX). Both will get the day-to-day notation tasks done and are available on both Mac and Windows platforms.

More advanced programs are Overture (Cakewalk), Encore (GVOX), Finale (Coda Music Systems), and Sibelius (Sibelius Software). They are all good, and continue to get better. No matter which notation program you choose, and no matter how easy-to-use the ads say they are, you will have to invest some time learning these programs. Investigate the literature in the ads, ask your friends, and see some demos. Then choose one, and stay with it. After you get the hang of it, you will be writing out parts with ease.

Music Utilities

The Music Maid (Signature Software) is a Mac-only product that is great for creating music worksheets fast! It is sometimes difficult to find, but is available through J. W. Pepper & Son. If you are a marching band instructor, you should check-out Pyware's two drill-design programs: 3D Dynamic Drill Design and Virtual 3D (both Windows and Mac).

Record Keeping

There are several dedicated programs for administration of a music department. Personally, I have had success using a generic database program called FileMaker Pro. It can be customized by the user for keeping records of anything imaginable. It can even do math functions (helpful when collecting money for fund-raisers), keep track of uniforms, music libraries, class lists, names, addresses, phone numbers, etc. It can sort lists in virtually any order and print them out. It is great for putting lists of students in the concert programs. (Create a text document of all students in alphabetical order and flow it right into your word processor.) It is available for both Mac and Windows.

Text/Page Layout

QuarkXpress (Quark) and PageMaker (Adobe Systems) are the two old-timers in this category. There are many others. These are great for creating great-looking concert programs. They are both capable of creating very polished and sophisticated print material. Even a word processor such as Microsoft Word can be a big help with programs, letters, or any print material where you want to present a professional image to the public.

Internet Browsers

If you are not yet accessing the Internet, you are missing one the most important resources of our time: the World Wide Web (WWW). Most new computers come bundled with an Internet browser. The three most popular are Netscape Communicator, Internet Explorer, and of course America-On-Line's (AOL) native browser. All three have e-mail capabilities built-in. If you have not yet made the leap to the Web, you should go ahead and jump right in. There is a tremendous amount of useful information available to you as a music teacher. You will not regret it.

As you can see, with your one computer, there are many useful activities for you and your students. This article only scratches the surface. Maybe someday soon, we will all have enough workstations to use with an entire class of students—at the same time. There is hope. With our one computer, we could send a budget request in an e-mail to the superintendent.

Note: One of the best music technology catalogs is available free to teachers from Lentine's Music, 844 N. Main Street, Akron, OH 44310; phone: 800-822-6752; Internet: www.lentine.com.

This article originally appeared in the Winter 2000 issue of Connecticut's CMEA News. Reprinted by permission.

Music Technology 101
Patrick Ware

Technology—it's everywhere we go. It is physically impossible to make the morning commute to school without having some contact with technology. However, it seems that many times the use of technology stops just inside the music room door once the teacher has turned on the lights.

Having taught in Virginia for the last six years, I worked my way through the technology competencies, and like many of you, most of the things I did in class did not readily apply to my own teaching. My goal here is to give you a few ideas that can be used in your classroom tomorrow. In most cases, there are other technological ways to do what I am suggesting. These ideas, however, should be readily accessible to even the most timid of technological novices.

Record Keeping and Grading

The most formidable task for the general music teacher is accurate and meaningful record keeping. It is difficult enough to keep up with the names and faces of 600, 300, or even 200 students, much less remember how each student did on a quiz or improvisation. Most school systems make use of one of the two major spreadsheet programs by Claris or Microsoft. If you have access to one of these programs, it is the next best thing to an actual grade-book program. Using the spreadsheet for record keeping does require some knowledge of spreadsheets. The most basic knowledge will allow you to do all of the things that I suggest.

If your school is on a nine-week quarter, you may see your students twice a week, and with 30 children in a class, you will need to create a spreadsheet that is approximately 25 vertical columns by 35 horizontal rows. I like to add more cells (the individual blocks for information) than needed to allow for extra comments and new students. Across the first row, enter the column headers; last name, first name, and the dates on which your class meets. In the first column, you can now enter the last names of the students in your class. In the second column, you can enter the first names of the students, making sure to line up the correct first and last name. If you put the names into your spreadsheet out of order, you can go back and have the program sort them for you. For those slightly more advanced, you can use the average function to maintain a running average of student grades after you have input that data.

Once you have done this you have four choices:

1. Save and print out your spreadsheet. The format will require you to print landscape as opposed to portrait. It is best to print two for every class so as to have one for taking attendance and the second for recording grades.
2. Save a copy and keep your computer running this program throughout the day. Take attendance from your computer, and immediately enter grades and/or comments into your spreadsheet.
3. A combination of the first two options. Record your information on the printed

copy and transfer to the computer at the end of the day.

4. The personal data assistant. If you have access to one of these handheld computers, you can do any of the preceding options without ever lifting a pen.

Student Composition

Technology has been defined as anything that makes life easier. You can create your own staff paper, even with limited resources. Open up a word processing document, depress the shift key and the underline key (to the right of the 0), and hold it down until you have five lines and four spaces. Print out as much as you need or run off as many copies as you need. The smaller point size you use the closer your staff lines will be. This may not seem to be a great use of technology, but you are now able to provide manuscript paper to every member of your class. Through the use of different point sizes and fonts you can also tailor the size of the staff to each grade level; larger print for primary and middle elementary and smaller

print for upper elementary and beyond.

Transcribe and Save

If you have access to one computer and any music writing software, transcribing class songs or the occasional melody becomes very simple for you or your students. After teaching the use of the program to one or more of your students you could then designate a "scribe" to record the day's work. This in itself could become an ongoing assessment in ear training. If you have your students develop melodies to accompany short stories or poems, you can use music writing software to transcribe, save, and reprint the ideas for use at a later date.

These are only a few the ways in which you can use technology in your classroom. Simple ideas can be improved upon and expanded with a little bit of creativity and a good user's manual.

This article originally appeared in the February 2002 issue of Virginia's VMEA Notes. *Reprinted by permission.*

The Camcorder in the Classroom: Forgotten Technology?
Kenneth White

In a world filled with rapidly changing technology, music teachers are bombarded with ads in professional magazines and by salesmen hawking the latest in high-tech equipment. There are so many technological advances "out there," each touted as the answer to teaching music, that even seasoned "techies" find it difficult to keep up. Hearing the horror stories about how quickly equipment and software can become obsolete, many teachers wonder about the wisdom of making high-dollar investments in technology that may be useless in the near future. Valuable time can be spent researching the right hardware and software, learning the parameters of the technology, and evaluating its worth (Hermanson & Kerfoot, 1994). It is no wonder that music teachers, hard-pressed for time, are tempted to avoid dealing with these complexities.

The search for a useful interactive tool for the classroom could start on more familiar ground, with the often overlooked camcorder. We have become a visual society, but "television's ability to teach has rarely been used" (Stanfil, 1994).

Before a spring concert several years ago, I looked into an audience of enthusiastic parents with video cameras trained on my every word and

every move. (Yikes!) They weren't trying to put me on national TV, of course, but wanted to tape their "little darlings" to view later as part of the family scrapbook of sorts. I asked my students to bring their videos the next day, and we watched the concert. I was amazed at how much more attentive they were than when listening to an audiotape of the concert, although the audiotape was of much better quality.

Videotaping classes and rehearsals also proved effective. The presence of the camera, regardless of whether the students were conscious of it, did little to change their behavior. It did, however, give me an opportunity to assess and modify my own behavior. On the tape, for example, I could immediately see and hear how many times I stopped the lesson. I could tell whether I had responded to a student positively or negatively. I could more easily judge the effectiveness of my rehearsal techniques (Berg & Smith, 1996).

The idea to use videotape tests quickly followed. Initially the students were apprehensive that other students might view the test video, but those concerns quickly faded. They soon realized that videotaping allowed them to pay attention to details that otherwise might go unnoticed. Posture, hand position, embouchure placement, and tone quality are just a few of the objectives that can be reviewed and tested in this way

(Stanfil, 1994). To extend the learning experience, students may critique other students' performances, but the teacher must set strict guidelines for peer evaluation so that no one's feelings are hurt.

Ultimately we decided to make a 15-minute recruitment video. All the students were involved in this production. The librarian's help was enlisted to record rehearsals, and the students practiced hard, knowing that many potential middle school band members would be watching. In addition to performance footage, the tape featured prepared and ad lib remarks ranging from the matter-of-fact ("This is a clarinet") to the personal (an eighth grader confessing how nervous he was when he first started in band and explaining how he overcame his fears). Because of our limited editing capabilities, the finished product contained imperfections, but we were all pleased and proud of it.

In videotaping music classes, the most important technical limitation is the built-in microphone, which is the weakest feature of any camcorder, no matter what brand. One of my initial goals was to teach tone quality, intonation, and the comparative listening that it takes to match pitch with other instrumentalists. The videotape sound quality is less than satisfactory for that purpose. One possible solution is to purchase a stereo hi-fi VCR (usually the ones with the RCA plugs in front!) and a small pre-amp, which good microphones must be plugged into before being patched to the VCR. (Of course, patch the video-out on the camcorder with the video-in on the VCR.) With good microphones this arrangement can produce audio of much better quality than even the most expensive cassette recorders.

Lots of great technology has recently come on the scene in music, but most is not suitable for use in a large classroom setting. Check out your library's video equipment—the kids know how to use it, and you'll be surprised how analytical students can be about their achievement when they see themselves on tape.

References

Hermanson, C., & Kerfoot, J. (1994). Technology assisted teaching—Is it getting results? *American Music Teacher,* 43(6), 21.

Stanfil, D. (1994). High tech today. *American Music Teacher,* 43(6), 8.

Berg, M. H., & Smith, J. (1996). Using videotapes to improve teaching. *Music Educators Journal,* (82)4, 31–37.

White, K. (1990). Band and videotape (Idea Bank). *Music Educators Journal,* 76(5), 42–43.

This article originally appeared in the Fall 1998 issue of the Georgia Music News. *Reprinted by permission.*

Section 2

 Technology
and
World Musics

 Section 2

Technology and World Musics

World Music on the World Wide Web: Web Authoring as an Alternative to Term Papers
James Frankel

Two years ago, I began teaching a world music course to eighth graders at the middle school where I teach. In order to get materials for my students, I did a great deal of research on the Internet about 32 different cultures, representing each continent. The amount of work was awesome; searching and downloading for hours to create course materials. The culminating project at the end of the quarter was a written report about a culture that makes up each student's family background. The report was two pages long and included a picture of the country's flag, most popular instrument, and people dressed in traditional costume. After receiving term paper after term paper that was quite frankly rather dull and tedious to read through, I realized that I was shortchanging my students with such a traditional form of assessment. The purpose of this project is to have students explore their own ethnic heritage through creating a Web site that describes the history, culture, and music of their family background. In my teaching experience, I have noticed that there is a serious lack of material available for music educators in regard to teaching world music. While there are some exceptional texts about world music, there is very little aimed at teaching it at the middle school level. The material that is available that is specifically geared for that age level treats the subject area quite lightly with very little attention to history and culture. For example, one text talks about the music of Africa in five short paragraphs with one hand-drawn picture of a "native" playing a drum.

My middle school is quite techno-minded. We currently have 40 G4 Power Macs in our computer labs, and each classroom has at least one G3 Power Mac. All classrooms are wired through a centrally based T1 connection to the Internet. The students learn Web authoring in sixth grade using Adobe PageMill under the guidance of our outstanding computer technology teacher, Mrs. Randy Freedman. This emphasis on technology made the suggestion of this project easily manageable. But why the Web over a traditional term paper?

The advantages of a Web page over a written paper are numerous. Here are but a few: students can include as many color images as they wish as opposed to just a few, students can include audio recordings of representative works from their specific culture, students can include video images of people dancing and making music, students can create hyperlinks throughout the text of their pages that connect to related Web sites. The power of the Internet and Web authoring is that it is only limited by imagination.

Outline of Curriculum Unit
About 6 weeks into the course, students are presented with the following outline for the Web site project.

Web Site Final Project
Now that we are a few weeks in to the course and you have an idea of what are the important facets of each culture's music (history, culture, dance, instruments), you should begin thinking about the cultures that are represented in your family. Ask your parents about your heritage if you do not already know. Choose a country from which your parents are from and think about the following questions:

• What is the name of the country?
• Where is it located?
• What language is spoken there?

- What is the name of the currency they use?
- What does their flag look like?
- What type of government do they have?
- Trace the history of the country.
- Were they ever ruled by another country?
- Have other cultures influenced theirs?
- Have they ever been involved in a war?
- What type of food do they eat?
- What products are they known for?
- What types of jobs do people have in the country?
- Are they primarily farmers? business people? craftsmen?
- What types of instruments are used in the folk music of that country?
- How does the folk music relate to the history of the country?
- Are the instruments used related to another country?
- What types of dances are typical of the culture?
- Are there any special holidays specific to the culture?
- How does the folk music sound?
- What does the popular music of that country sound like? Is it like ours?
- What makes you proud about being from that country?
- Why did your ancestors move to America?
- What is one thing about your culture that you would like to see as a part of ours?

There are a lot of deep questions here. Think about them. Ask your parents or grandparents about your culture. Once you have thought about the 20 questions listed above, develop an outline for a Web site that will portray your country's music for all to see. You will develop a Web site that will be attached to the school Web site. Think about the layout of the site. Think about links. Think about using images, videos, and sound clips. Submit your outline for approval so you can begin creating your site.

Research Begins

Two weeks after this handout is distributed, students will be scheduled into one of our computer labs for a one week block so that they can begin researching their heritage. I will help the students out with some tips for searching the Web. I will tell the students to just put in the name of the country they are researching perhaps even adding the word "music" to their search. Students will then need to search through countless sites which contain the name

of their country, many having little to do with music, culture, or history. Students will need to act as their own filter of what is valuable and what is not. There are numerous sites on tourism of the different countries, and these are some of the best sites for pictures and even videos. Again, students need to be aware that these are usually commercial sites with profit on their minds. When a student enters "Israel Music" into a search engine, they will find many commercial music Web sites selling Israeli music. Many of these sites are strictly popular music and contain no resources on the history and culture, or folk music for that matter. Again, students need to discern what is valuable on them. The best sites that I have found on the Web for the music, culture, and history of different countries are usually produced by college and graduate students around the country. By adding .edu to the search, students can refine their results dramatically. This would be one of the searching tips that would also be related to the students. It would, of course, be wonderful if the students could find that out for themselves.

Once the students start finding some relevant Web sites about their countries, the next step will be for them to determine which are valuable and which are not. The assignment for the students after the first day of research in the lab will be to show their parents what they have found on the Web. Having their parents serve as secondary filters of information will not only be valuable for the student; the interaction of parent and child using the Web might foster a discussion about their culture or even about using the Internet for research in general. While it is certainly true that there is a fair share of garbage on the Internet, there is also a vast amount of valuable information. Just because it's published on the net doesn't make it a reliable source. Is it a .com, .edu, or .org? Does that make a difference? These are certainly things to consider whenever teachers assign a Web research project.

Students will save their research and the various audio and visual images they have found in their personal folders that are on the school server. The teacher will check the progress of the students' research in order to know when to proceed to the next step, design.

Designing the Site

Students have several tasks to complete in order to achieve a well designed Web site. These include finding the various forms of media discussed earlier to best illustrate their culture. Once students find this material on the Web, as well as text-based information, students will begin thinking about the design of the site. Using the Web evaluation form that I used to evaluate different Web sites, students will spend a class period looking at different Web sites about the music of their country and critically analyze the structure and design of the site. They will answer questions concerning the layout, organization, navigation, and the overall "look" of the site. They will articulate what they think makes a good site, and a bad one. After critiquing a few sites, students will open the organizational software Inspiration to create their site hierarchy trees. Students will then save their hierarchy trees to their personal folders. The teacher will then check to make sure that each student has completed their research and design for their site.

Specifications for Web Site

The following is the handout that students will receive prior to their creating the actual Web site. This handout also includes the grading procedure.

Expectations for World Music Web Site

Now that you have done some research and design for your final Web site project, it's time to know exactly what I expect from your Web site. The most important expectation is to completely avoid plagiarism. You are welcome to paraphrase the information that you find on the Internet, but remember, if you found it, so can I. Remember to focus on the 20 questions that were distributed on the last handout. Use them as a guide for what to talk about in the text portion of your site. If you find other interesting information contained on one of the sites you found, by all means include it, just don't copy it word for word. Enough said.

Here are the requirements for an A:
1. Answer the 20 questions.
2. Include images that illustrate the text, the more the better.
3. Create at least 10 hyperlinks embedded into the text for further exploration.
4. Include at least one audio example.
5. Site can be made up of numerous pages or one continuous cascading page. If you choose to cascade, be sure to include a menu or navigation tool at the top of the page so that users do not need to scroll through all of the information.
6. Create a clear navigation system.

7. Create a links page to other exemplary Web sites on your topic.
8. Use tables to organize your information.
9. Create frames if you know how.
10. Test the site.
11. Make sure it works.
12. What browser plug-ins are required?
13. Be sure to include links to download any that might not be available to the user.

To receive a grade lower than an A, you will have to leave out some of items 1 through 7. Items 8, 9 and 10 are optional. The more you leave out, the lower your grade. Remember, this is a project that is intended for you to learn more about your family's history, culture, and music. Creating a Web site is just applying your existing knowledge to create something that many people will see and learn from.

Creation of Web Site

Once the students have submitted a design that meets the requirements, they will begin to create their sites. Using Adobe PageMill, they will spend the next week in the computer lab actually constructing their sites. The teacher and the computer lab administrator will monitor student progress and help with technical as well as design questions. Once the students have created their sites, they will use the FTP program Fetch, which they are all familiar with, to publish their sites to the school Web site. Their sites will be located in the music portion of the site. While the size of their Web sites is certainly a concern, especially when they contain video and audio, our school server space is immense and should not pose a problem.

Presentation of Final Projects

Once all of the sites are up on the Internet, the students will present their projects to the class, much as they would if they were presenting their written reports orally. Students will not discuss how they created the Web sites at all. Here, the media is not the message, the content is. Students will present their cultures to the class and give a tour of their site and what kinds of artifacts it contains. Students will also assess each others' work using both the 20 questions from the first handout and the expectations handout as a scoring rubric. They can comment on the design of the site as well. The teacher will also use both handouts as a rubric. Students will be graded on both their research and their Web site development, with more weight on research.

Implementation

Before entering the computer lab to begin working on their Web sites, the students had submitted the overall design of their Web site and had done research on their own to answer the questions that were distributed. Research and design is a time-consuming process, time which we simply did not have in the computer lab. When the students arrived at the computer lab, they were well prepared for the task at hand.

On Monday, October 10, 2001, the students in the eighth grade general music class went to the computer lab in our school for a brief review on using Adobe PageMill to create Web pages. The students reviewed how to create backgrounds, tables, links to other pages within the Web site, links to other pages on the Internet, inserting pictures, clip art, video, and sound. On Tuesday, the students created the basic structure of their Web sites and made sure that the links within their site worked. Students also created their home pages and the navigational menus. Both the computer teacher and myself assisted students by answering any questions they might have had about the technical aspects of Web site design and construction. The students had very few problems with the technical aspects of the project. Most had questions about where to find reliable information and pictures on the Internet.

On Wednesday, the students began to fill in the rest of their Web sites with the answers to the questions they were given previously. They also began to include the various images and sounds that they were able to locate on the Internet. Thursday was spent refining their Web sites and testing them in both Internet Explorer and Netscape Navigator for browser conflicts. Finally, on Friday, the students uploaded their completed Web sites to the school server. This can be a time-consuming process if the Web sites are not well organized, but the students did a great job designing their Web sites so it was quite easy. By the end of class, all of the Web sites were up and running on our school Web site.

Results

Overall, the results of this assessment project were excellent. The students expressed their enjoyment of completing such a project, which serves as an alternative to the traditional term paper. Almost all of the students had little to no difficulty in designing and building their Web sites. Those students who expressed some concern about the technical aspects of the project were paired with students who felt comfortable with the technology involved. In my period 4 class I had 18 students who completed 10 Web site projects. In my period 5 class, I had 18 students who completed 12 Web site projects. The scoring of the projects can be broken down as follows: 11 groups received a score of A; 6 groups received a score of A-; 4 groups received a score of B+; and 1 group received a score of C+. It should be noted that my particular school does not award A+ to any student work, in any subject area.

Of the 17 groups that received a score of A or A-, each Web site was well designed and executed. The groups that received an A- did not include enough information about the culture of their particular country. The students agreed with the score they received because of the clearly delineated scoring rubric. The 4 groups that received a score of B+ had varying reasons for a lower score. Two groups did not include any audio examples, which was one of the mandatory requirements of the project. One group included very little information about the music of their chosen country although the rest of the information on their Web site was complete. The remaining group received a B+ because they did not include any links to other relevant Web sites, which was a mandatory requirement of the project. The group that received a score of C+ included very little information about the history and culture of their chosen country.

Evaluation of Project

This project involved a great deal of logistical planning on the part of the teacher, including making arrangements for computer lab time, and extensive research on what was available to the students online before assigning them the project. As stated earlier, there is a great deal of information on the Internet, only a small percentage of which is actually reliable. In order to ensure that the students had a positive experience with a strong opportunity for success, it was necessary to do a great deal of online research outside of class. I also researched other student-created Web sites, especially those created by the students of Dr. Cecilia Wong, who teaches at the University of Kentucky and includes this activity as part of her curriculum for a class she teaches which focuses on teaching world music.

It is certainly easier to assign students a term paper with a list of requirements than to assign them a Web site project. There is little, if any, work that the teacher needs to complete while the students are in the research and writing process. The major time aspect in such an assessment project is actually reading the student work. This time factor does not disappear when assigning a Web site project. In fact, grading the student work on a Web site takes far more time than grading a traditional term paper. However, in talking to the students after completing the project, all of the students felt that completing a Web site in place of a term paper was far more interesting to them. Many also commented that they liked using the knowledge that they had on computers in a different subject area. The other factor about the project that most of the students enjoyed was that their work was included on the school Web site for their families and friends to see. Usually with term papers, my experience is that they throw their work in the garbage as soon as they receive their grade. With the Web site, their work is displayed on a very large, public "refrigerator."

I strongly believe that the extra effort and time involved in developing and administering this assessment project is well worth it. For the first time in the 9 years I have been teaching general music, my students were actually excited about completing a final term project. The administrators in my building as well as the superintendent of schools were delighted with the results, noting that it was good to see that the technology in the school was being put to good use. I plan on administering this assessment project as part of my permanent general music curriculum, and I would recommend other general music teachers do the same, or at least explore the possibility of doing so.

This article originally appeared in the January 2002 issue of New Jersey's Tempo. *Reprinted by permission.*

The Internet: A Connection to World Musics
C. Victor Fung

In this age of telecommunication, the use of the Internet has exploded in almost all types of businesses, educational institutions, major cities, and even small towns in developed countries. The Internet has become a vigorous and viable medium that connects to information about various aspects of life throughout the world. Internet technology helps break through distance barriers, and in the United States, access to the Internet is available in many, if not the vast majority of, homes, schools, and offices. With some careful considerations, music educators may make use of the Internet to connect their teaching practices with musical cultures from around the world despite the distance and the lack of knowledge and training in certain musical cultures. Both teachers and learners can learn about various musical cultures through materials available on the Internet.

In the past few years, music education programs in the United States, and in some other countries, have included more world music components than ever. This trend seems set to continue into the foreseeable future. From preservice teacher training, to in-service workshops, to programs emphasizing research, many of these programs have shared an interest in world musics. This implies a sharp increase in demand for world music materials for a teacher's classroom use or

professional development. Many publishers, such as MENC: The National Association for Music Education and the World Music Press, have produced valuable materials for music teachers in world musics.

In addition to the hard copies of books, lesson plans, teaching tools, and accessories and various forms of single medium and multimedia recordings, the Internet provides a fast-growing body of world music materials for music teachers. These materials are growing by the minute. The aim of this article is to point out some world music materials available on the Internet and some of their applications for music teachers.

Considerations
The foremost consideration in using the Internet is validity of information. Current Web-authoring technology allows almost anyone to post information on a Web page. As one surfs on the Web, one seldom questions who the author of a Web site is. If no author or organization endorses a Web page, music teachers should view the page with considerable skepticism and use informed judgements on the validity of the information posted, including the music sound files. If an author or organization endorses a Web page, measures must be used to ensure that they are credible. Organizations comprised of music professionals and expert scholars tend to provide valid and reliable information.

The second consideration in using the Internet relates to the speed of growth and change in the

Internet. Thousands of new Web sites are being created every day, and many more of them are being updated, inactivated, or relocated. Teachers must have a contingency plan if a Web site being used is not current anymore and should have other Web sites or other activities planned in case a specific Web site is no longer accessible.

The third consideration concerns the nature of information available from the Internet and the educational goals determined by the teacher. All Internet materials and activities used must parallel the level of student learning and educational goals. Sometimes new materials available from the Internet are so attractive that teachers may loose sight of their educational goals. When teachers believe that materials available on the Internet are valid and can meet some educational goals, they may utilize these materials in their music teaching.

Applications for Music Teachers

Music teachers can use world music materials available on the Internet for students' learning (in-class activities or assignments) or for themselves (professional development or research for purchases). Many Web sites can benefit both the teacher's development and the students' learning.

In-class activities. Various settings can be used in a music class depending on the educational goal and the number of computers available in the classroom. If there is only one computer, I highly recommend a projection system and a sound amplification system. The whole class can view various Web pages and listen to downloadable music files. In addition, students can take turns sharing their Web pages with the whole class. If there are multiple computers in the classroom (i.e., students work in small groups or individually with a computer), more flexible arrangements are possible. A teacher can set each computer on a different Web site, and students, in groups or individually, rotate to a different computer for a different Web site. This can help students to stay on task without taking the time to search or load specific Web sites. Another arrangement could be having each computer set to a different Web site, and students can share verbally with the whole class what they find. A third arrangement is to have everyone looking at the same Web site at a given time. In this case, the teacher should be aware of the possible delays due to limited host-server capacity; that is, not every computer in the classroom can load the same Web site at the same pace if they can

be loaded onto multiple computers simultaneously at all.

Assignments. Students may use designated Web sites as resources to complete a task. Teachers should keep in mind that Web sites are not the only resources for all assignments, and students should be made aware of it, too. Among the many advantages of using the Internet for assignments, students can work individually at their own pace. In addition, students can share their working process with parents and siblings if they work on their assignments at home, or they can share their working process with their peers if they work on their assignments at school.

Professional development. There are many Web sites that provide a vast amount of information about various types of world musics. The list of these Web sites is basically unlimited. I would recommend music teachers use various search engines (e.g., ask.com) to look for a specific musical tradition or a specific musical genre. Paralleled with the large explosion of the Internet, Web sites concerning various types of world musics also exploded. With patience, persistence, and an open mind, one could find it rewarding to learn about world musics on the Internet. Perhaps one might be motivated to examine a musical culture more seriously.

Research for purchases. As in any kind of business, many vendors in world musics have Web sites designed for customers. Music teachers can use these Web sites to find out more details, including features and prices, about any products they want to use in their music teaching. These products include single medium and multimedia recordings, books, musical instruments, computer software, and teaching tools and accessories. Using some search engines, music teachers may even be able to contact musicians nearby who may provide a service to visit your school.

With these four uses of the Internet in mind (i.e., in-class activities, assignments, professional development, and research for purchases), many of the Web sites in the first three categories are interchangeable, depending on the level of student learning and the nature of the educational goals. Figures 1 and 2 present some Web site examples that might serve one or more of these purposes. Some of these Web sites focus on a specific musical tradition (figure 1), while others provide links to multiple musical traditions (figure 2). Figure 3 presents Web sites directed towards music teachers who would like to find more resources and purchase some world music materials. All Web sites presented in this article are examples only, and they are current as of the time of writing this article. There are many more to be discovered and to be created. The world of music is open for exploration in the world of the Internet in convenient and speedy ways.

This article first appeared in the May–June 2000 issue of Ohio's TRIAD. *Reprinted by permission.*

Figure 1
Sample Web Sites Focusing on a Specific Musical Tradition

African Music Home Page	www.africanmusic.com
Free Drum Lessons and Hand Drum Rhythms Notation Online	www.life-free.net/cougar/rhythm.htm
Ceolas Celtic Music Archive	www.ceolas.org/ceolas.html
Le Gamelan en France	http://gamelan.citeweb.net/liste.htm
Bali & Beyond	www.pacificnet.net/gamelan/
Gagaku Home Page	www.gagaku.net/index.ENG.html
Kabuki for Everyone	www.fix.co. jp/kabuki/kabuki.html
Japanese Flutes	www.asahi-net.or. jp/~dlls-ymgc/index-e.htm
Shakuhachi—Traditional Japanese bamboo flute	www.shakuhachi.com/home.html
Koto: Japanese Traditional Music Instrument	www.asahi-net.or. jp/~np5y-hruc/kt-koto.html
The Internet Chinese Music Archive	http://metalab.unc.edu/pub/multimedia/chinese-music/
Chinese Lion Dance	www.umich.edu/~karatedo/AMAS/LionDance/liondance.html
ChinaSite.com: Chinese Music—The Complete Reference to the Web Sites of Chinese Music	http://ChinaSite.com/ChinaMusic.html
Musical Malaysia	www.music.upm.edu.my/malaysia/index.html
What Is [Angklung]?	http://members.xoom.com/angklung/html/what_is.html

Figure 2
Sample Web Sites Providing Links to Multiple Musical Traditions

The World of Music	http://library.thinkquest.org/11315/
Worldwide Internet Music Resources: Genres	www.music.indiana.edu/music_resources/genres.html
Center for World Music: Links	www.centerforworldmusic.org/links.html
Ethnomusicology	www.lib.washington.edu/music/world.html
World Music Links	www.rootsworld.com/wmce/wmlinks.html
Ethnomusicology	www.zinezone.com/zines/music/world/ethnomusic/index.html

Figure 3
Sample Web Sites Directed Toward Teachers

Professional Development: Ethnic and Multicultural Music Page	www.cmeabaysection.org/ethnic.html
Multicultural Education and Ethnic Groups: Selected Sources	www.library.csustan.edu/lboyer/multicultural/main.htm
Research for Purchase: World Music Store	http://secure.vscape.net/acb/webpage.cfm ?WebPage_ID=1&DID=12
World Music Press	www.worldmusicpress.com/

Section 3

 # Using Internet Technology

 Section 3

Using Internet Technology

WebQuest: A Valuable Teaching Tool in General Music
Susan Chunn

Teaching is often like a jigsaw puzzle with many pieces to be put together before the puzzle is complete and success is achieved. Likewise, a teacher must constantly combine numerous variables in problem solving to achieve student learning. This represents one of the biggest challenges in the teaching profession. Recently, as an elementary general music teacher preparing to introduce opera to my students, I was faced with the following "puzzle pieces."

• The National Standards for Music Education— Content Standard 9 (Understanding music in relation to history and culture)[1]
• A Cleveland Opera on Tour miniresidency performance of *The Barber of Seville* for the 900 fourth- and fifth-grade students in our school
• My 375 fifth-grade general music students at our school
• Limited teaching time with these students
• A push to integrate curricula and technology into the teaching/learning
• A need to differentiate instruction for these students
• A need for a manageable means to assess their learning

How did I put together this "puzzle"? I created a WebQuest, a teacher-created Web site. [Note: Chunn's WebQuest can be found at http://wneo.org/WebQuests/TeacherWebQuests/barber/barber.htm.

Teacher-Created Web Site
A WebQuest is a Web site created by a teacher for his or her own students, usually in the intermediate grades or above. Bernie Dodge, professor of educational technology at San Diego State University, created the WebQuest concept in 1995.[2] A WebQuest is similar to most any kind of lesson plan. It provides an introduction, objectives, materials, a process, an evaluation, and a conclusion. A WebQuest is made up of specific building blocks. Upon changing the building blocks, a teacher can accomplish most any learning goal. By visiting this specific teacher-created Web site, students are (1) introduced to a topic, (2) given tasks related to that topic, (3) provided with the guidance and resources needed to accomplish these tasks, (4) given an explanation of the type of evaluation to be used by the teacher, and (5) provided with a summary and an extension of the lesson goals.[3] A big advantage of WebQuests is that they can provide work for students at school or at home, in groups or individually. Through the use of this computer technology, many variables can be combined so that learning may be achieved.

The Barber of Seville WebQuest
For my students, I created a WebQuest entitled *The Barber of Seville*. The WebQuest began with an introduction intended to spike my students' interest, including a brief description of and historical background on comic opera.

Next, students were given a choice of 4 learning tasks to pursue. One task was to write a descriptive comparison of a video excerpt of the opera shown in music class to the live Cleveland Opera on Tour performance given at our school. A second task was to research the history of barbering, interview a present-day barber, and then compare this information in a written report. A third choice was to make a collage of pictures from the opera or draw, paint, or sketch pictures that retell the story. The pictures could be the original work of the student or could come from Internet links provided in the WebQuest. Another choice was to listen to music from the opera on the Internet or from recordings and then learn to play one of the melodies by ear on an instrument. The student would then perform the melody for me at school.

I included very specific directions for accomplishing each task, giving Web sites that were direct links to many resources. I explained how the tasks would be evaluated. I concluded by suggesting that students might gain a greater understanding and appreciation of opera and might attend other operas in the future after completing the WebQuest. Throughout the Web site I used various fonts, pictures, and graphics to make the Web site appealing to my students, just as anyone might do in creating an interesting Web page.

Completing the Puzzle

Through the use of this Web site, I was able to combine all of the variables to complete my puzzle. First, my students were able to experience a live performance of *The Barber of Seville* presented by Cleveland Opera on Tour and assisted by our school's fifth-grade select choir. Their miniresidency consisted of a workshop for music teachers and two rehearsals at our school led by the tour's professionals. A daytime and evening performance of the opera concluded the residency. Before the performances, I presented an introductory lesson in music class.

After the performances, I assigned all my students *The Barber of Seville* WebQuest for homework. This homework addressed the problem of limited teaching time. It also connected the learning with computer technology, other curricula, and extended the learning to my students' homes. To meet National Standard 9,[4] I broadened my students' knowledge and experience with the libretto, the characters, and the music of the opera by guiding them toward various preselected Web sites where they could read about, view scenes, and listen to music from the opera.

The next puzzle piece was more difficult to place. To differentiate instruction for 375 students seemed like a monumental task. However, in the book *The Differentiated Classroom—Responding to the Needs of All Learners,* author Carol Ann Tomlinson defines differentiation of instruction as a teacher's response to learners' needs guided by general principles of differentiation such as respectful tasks, flexible groupings, and/or ongoing assess-

ment and adjustments. Teachers can differentiate the content, process, or product of an assignment according to students' readiness, interest, and learning profile through a multitude of instructional and management strategies.[5] This allows students the opportunity to build on prior knowledge and skills as well as personal interests and strengths.

So for my instruction, I developed a varied array of tasks related to *The Barber of Seville* from which the students could select their homework. I created these task ideas after visiting another Web site authorized by Bernie Dodge, "WebQuest Taskonomy, a Taxonomy of Tasks." In this Web site, Dodge compiled a list of common task formats used in WebQuests from which I selected the components the Retelling Task, the Compilation Task, the Journalistic Task, the Design Task, the Creative Product Tasks and the Judgement Task.[6] Using these different tasks, I could:

- Blend assessment and instruction.
- Allow students to begin learning where they are.
- Allow students to work with appropriately challenging tasks.
- Allow modification of working conditions based on learning style.
- Avoid work that is anxiety producing or boredom producing.
- Promote success and therefore, motivate.[7]

Bloom's Taxonomy

Additionally, through these tasks, students could employ varying levels of thinking skills to complete their assignment. An example of such thinking skills is the work of Dr. Benjamin Bloom of the University of Chicago. His work, known as Bloom's taxonomy, includes the skills [in the cognitive domain] of knowledge, comprehension, application, analysis, synthesis and evaluation.[8] The collage/art task allowed for a display of knowledge, comprehension, application, analysis, and/or synthesis as they identified, explained, and made their own pictures to show me they knew the story and its characters. The musical task involved application and analysis as they applied musical memory and technical skills to arrive at a form for the musical presentation and discovered specific pitches to recreate a melody line. For the written reports, students synthesized and evaluated in their comparisons of the taped and live performances and of the barbering profession as it has changed over many years.

Theory of Multiple Intelligences

Furthermore, this particular set of tasks supports

the multiple intelligences theory of Dr. Howard Gardner (Harvard University) who has identified 8 separate human intelligences.[9] These assignments stressed the use of six of those intelligences. The task of learning to play a melody from the opera by ear on an instrument uses the musical and kinesthetic intelligences. Creating a collage/art work uses the spatial intelligence. Writing a report uses the linguistic intelligence. Interviewing a barber uses one's interpersonal intelligence. Just choosing the task, doing one's best work, and turning it in on time uses one's intrapersonal intelligence. These tasks seemed to meet the needs of all of my students and they seemed eager to do their homework using their own strengths and interests.

Assessing the Projects

One of the most overwhelming parts of completing this puzzle was the assessment of all of these projects. William E. Loadman, education professor at The Ohio State University, suggests to teachers that one of their responsibilities is to provide students with meaningful and useful assessments that assist students with their learning. He believes providing multiple assessments is a powerful classroom strategy to facilitate student learning. Among his list of multiple assessments is project-based learning. He suggests that these project-based produces be assessed using a rubric.[10] My students offered ideas that helped me to develop the rubric used for evaluating their WebQuest projects.[11] (See figure 1.)

Learning Goal Accomplished

When my students turned in their projects, they did so with a strong sense of ownership and pride. They had enjoyed doing their homework and it showed in the extraordinary quality of their work. I definitely felt my teaching goal had been accomplished. With little teaching time, my students gained understanding of an opera.

Through their search of the resources, they saw this opera in relation to the time period and the culture. With the choices of tasks, they were able to work according to their strengths and interests. They knew how they would be assessed, and most were able to do their work on their home computers.

Through the Cleveland Opera on Tour miniresidency and their WebQuest assignments, they gained a new appreciation for opera as an art form. Producing a good WebQuest could allow students to achieve success with virtually any learning goal. From my personal experience, I highly recommend the WebQuest as a valuable teaching tool, and I hope that other general music teachers may find success with its use.

References

1. Consortium of National Arts Education Associations. (1994). *National Standards for Arts Education*. Reston, VA: MENC, p. 45.

2. Dodge, Bernie. "Some Thoughts About WebQuest." http://edweb.sdsu.edu/courses/edtec596/about_webquests.html. November 15, 2001.

Figure 1. Rubric for WebQuest

	Excellent	Good	Satisfactory	Needs Improvement
Creativity	Original and unique project	Much evidence of creativity	Little evidence of creativity	No evidence of creativity
Application	Applied knowledge in original way	Much evidence of knowledge application	Little evidence of knowledge application	No knowledge application
Directions	All directions followed	Most directions followed	Few directions followed	No directions followed
Neatness	Extremely well-organized or rehearsed	Much attempt to organize or rehearse	Little attempt to organize or rehearse	No organization or rehearsal
Timeliness	Turned in by due date	Turned in one day past due date	Turned in after homework notice	Turned in after phone call home

3. Dodge, Bernie. "Building Blocks of a WebQuest." http://edweb.sdsu.edu/people/bdodge/webquest/buildingblocks.html. January 23, 2001.

4. Consortium of National Arts Education Associations. (1994). *National Standards for Arts Education.* Reston, VA: MENC, p. 45.

5. Tomlinson, Carol Ann. (1999). *The Differentiated Classroom: Responding to the Needs of All Learners.* Association for Supervision and Curriculum Development, p. 15.

6. Dodge, Bernie. "WebQuest Taskonomy: A Taxonomy of Tasks." http://edweb.sdsu.edu/webquest/taskonomy.html. January 23, 2001.

7. Tomlinson, Carol Ann (1995). *How to Differentiate Instruction in Mixed Ability Classrooms.* Association for Supervision and Curriculum Development, Appendix.

8. Clark, Barabar (1979). *Growing Up Gifted,* 2nd ed. Charles Merrill Publishing Company, pp. 195–196, 222.

9. Gardner, Howard. (1993). *Multiple Intelligences: The Theory into Practice—A Reader.* Basic Books, pp. 13–29.

10. Loadman, William E. (2001). "Helping Students: Using Assessment to Facilitate Learning." *Ohio Schools,* 79(4) pp. 11–13.

11. High Plains Regional Technology in Education Consortium. "Create Rubrics for Your Project-Based Learning Activities." http://rubistar.4teachers.org. Sept. 20, 2001.

This article originally appeared in the April 2002 issue of Ohio's TRIAD. *Reprinted by permission.*

One Computer and 24 Students
Jennifer Jakubowski

As a teacher, I want my students to utilize the Listening Project Web pages and the Internet in general. There is information on the Internet that I cannot show my students any other way. For example, you can see Mozart's house in Austria. That is a great way to connect students with composers and their lifestyles. My dilemma was, how do I get a class of 24 students to effectively use my one computer with Internet access?

Assuming you have Internet access in your classroom or through a network, there are two ways you can do this. Students can use the Internet for an "information treasure hunt" with a worksheet, or they can use it as a research tool with a finished product. In order to accomplish this second idea, I proposed that my students create a Big Book of the Listening Project Compositions, with a page on each composition. The Internet was the research tool for the page.

In order to have students effectively do research on my one computer with Internet access, I broke the class into stations. The class of 24 was broken into 6 groups of 4, and I assigned each group one of the Listening Project compositions to research.

I had 6 stations set up around my room where one group of students remained for one entire music class. Examples of stations are—computer with Internet access, another computer with Music Ace 2, keyboards, listening center, and an instrument station where students create accompaniments to a poem or a play.

At the computer with Internet, the students' job was to research their composition. They used the Listening Project Web Pages to do this. I provided them with a packet that contained questions to guide their research. In the packet there was a composer page, where students went to a site about the composer, read about his life, and wrote down interesting facts to eventually put in their book page. Students went to Web sites and researched one or more relevant instruments from their composition. I allowed students to print pictures from the Internet. These pictures became another form of research for their book page. The students were excited to find "cool" pictures for their page. Some of the pictures included were—composer pictures, instrument pictures, maps of composers' countries of origin, and other relevant pictures relating to their compositions (e.g., a dancer doing the cancan for the composition *Can-Can*).

After the stations were completed, the students then assembled their research into a page for a Big Book. I gave the students two class periods to create their book page. Glue, scissors, poster board, and markers were provided—the rest was their imagination. I played all of the Listening Project compositions as they worked. It was great to see them dig into their work as their song was being played!

After students created their pages, I laminated all of them and assembled them into a book. Students then presented their page to the class. By doing this, the students really took ownership of their composition. They are always eager to show others what they know, and they really did know a lot!

This is one way to integrate the Internet into the music classroom. If time is too tight to create a book, provide students with a research page or worksheet in which they use the Listening Project Web Pages as a treasure map. Students can go to various sites to find answers to questions such as "Where was Gliere born?" "What instruments did he play?" "Were any members of his family musicians?" The worksheet could be done with an entire class in a lab. I've found students love to use the Internet, but don't always realize how much they can learn from it.

There are many ways to integrate the Internet into the music classroom. Hopefully I've given you some ideas that will work for you!

This article originally appeared in the December 2001 issue of the Wisconsin School Musician. *Reprinted by permission.*

Music on the Web: Basics of Why and How to Use the New Internet Audio Technologies
Dave Sebald

Like many commercial enterprises, an ever growing number of school music organizations have been exploring the benefits of creating their own Web sites. After all, a large part of any music department's extra-instructional function is public relations, and, as the world of commerce has discovered, no current medium has as long a PR reach or as broad a multimedia potential as the World Wide Web. Today, anyone, anywhere in the world who has an interest in our music programs and a connection to the Internet can immediately access any information we want to publish. In addition to basic identity pages, many school music organizations publish mission statements, performance schedules, ensemble handbooks, histories, award lists, and other motivational information. Text, photos, and wonderfully creative graphics abound on these sites. What doesn't abound on most school music sites yet is music—or audio in any form!

Why Web Audio?
Technically, sound has lagged far behind other media on the Web primarily because it is a time-based form of communication and requires greater continuous bandwidth than text or images. Even a window-filling, information-rich picture posted on a Web site rarely exceeds 30,000 bytes in size, but until recently, the same number of bytes would provide only a few seconds of listenable audio—certainly not enough to represent our art well. Until recently, digital sound has required more numbers than could be pulled through the technologies that make up the Internet.

But now the paradigm is changing. The analog modem technologies that were most peoples' link to the Internet only a few years ago are fast giving way to digital technologies like DSL and cable modems. At the same time, new refinements of file compression algorithms are lowering the amount of data required to create listenable audio. While it may still be in its infancy, quality Web-based sound is now a real possibility to those willing to take the time needed to understand it.

Web audio requires digitized sound, and luckily, the above-mentioned advances in Web technologies have been accompanied by similar leaps in digital recording technologies. Only a few years ago, digital audio was solely the province of expensive and highly specialized studios. Today any personal computer is capable of producing CD-quality digital sound files. Devices like mini-CD recorders have made capturing sound in the digital domain easy, unobtrusive, and far less expensive than old analog devices.

The educational paradigm is changing too. Easy access to high-end recording technology has spawned a keen interest among students in this aspect of our art. Many students are now as interested in learning how to produce music as they are in how to perform it. Although this shift may seem intimidating to a traditionalist, it is a trend that should not be ignored by music educators but rather embraced as an effective and motivating avenue for reinforcing musical concepts.

Web audio's potential for instruction is as enormous as it has been for public relations. The Web is, after all, a form of publication—a means of widely disseminating anything people want to communicate, including images and sound. Currently the most ubiquitous audio application among schools is for putting representative ensemble performances on the Web site, but the instructional possibilities extend beyond that. Here are just a few alternative ideas:

- Commented solo and ensemble performances
- Student computer compositions
- Student recorded performances
- Narrated educational presentations by the directors
- Student narrated presentations on musical concepts
- Streaming audio radio station

Notice from the above list that Web audio can be more than just another public relations device: it can be a very effective motivator and educational tool as well.

Do It Yourself

If the possibilities intrigue you, you'll be happy to know that it is neither expensive nor difficult to implement them. These are the tools you need:

1. **Sound recorder.** This doesn't have to be digital—your computer can digitize analog input easily—but it should be high quality. The file compression processes necessary for putting audio on the Web will degrade the audio to a certain degree so it makes sense to start with the best-quality source material possible. The new mini-CD recorders are inexpensive ($200–$300) and produce near CD quality recordings when used correctly. While perhaps not as high caliber as DAT, their output is far better than the reel-to-reel and cassette formats they were created to replace. In a pinch it is possible to use a hi-fi VHS recorder for audio; the sound is remarkably good. It is also possible to forego the recording device entirely and record directly to a computer's hard drive with the software mentioned below. However, this option is usually not as convenient. In any case, care should be taken to use the best microphones available and to choose as good and as quiet a recording environment as possible.

2. **Sound digitizer/editor.** Any fast computer with a good sound card and a large hard drive will do this. My home Windows PC contains only a 450 MHz Athlon chip and a 6 GB hard drive. The sound card is a $99 Sound Blaster Live which includes a very capable digital sound editor, Sound Forge XP.

   This combination works fine for digitizing sound from my mini-CD and for producing final compressed files for the Web. Cool Edit LE is a popular alternative to Sound Forge on the PC. For work outside my house I use a Mac 500 MHz PowerBook running Sound Edit 16 or sometimes BIAS Peak LE.

   It is worth mentioning here that one of the most respected pieces of digital audio software, Digidesign's Pro Tools, is available in a free ver-

sion as a download from www.digidesign.com. Available for Windows 98 and ME (not 2000 yet) and for Macintosh OS 9 (not X yet). It represents the best software value around for digitizing and editing sound.

3. **Web page editor.** Any current Web page editor works for linking audio to a clickable word or image. Two of the most popular for either Mac or PC are Macromedia's Dreamweaver. and Microsoft's FrontPage. Dreamweaver features the ability to download extensions from the Macromedia Web site that make embedding audio into Web pages much easier. In the event that no Web page editor is available, any word processor that can save files in ASCII text format (.txt) will also work. Web pages are really nothing more than a set of verbal directions that Web browsers like Internet Explorer and Netscape Navigator interpret to format page layouts. Many Web page builders actually prefer hand coding these directions. They are called HTML for HyperText Markup Language.

4. **Web hosting service.** In order to appear on the Internet, a server that hosts Web pages must be identified by a unique numerical address and a domain name in a form like www.utsa.edu. Almost all school districts in Texas now possess these addresses, so it should not be a problem to request that your district's network administrator give you space on the Web server's hard drive, assign it a subname like www.utsa.edu/multimedia, and tell you how to upload and download files to it. It is also possible in many instances to assign a unique number and domain name directly to your site as in http://multimedia.utsa.edu. The amount of space required for audio files will be larger than for simple Web pages—probably more than 20 MB. However, if this becomes an issue, the space requirement can be lowered by regularly deleting old audio files as others become more current. Luckily, most schools think that the PR value of advanced Web techniques like audio outweighs the speed and space requirements they demand.

How To Do It

Although it is beyond the scope of this article to present a tutorial on Web page creation, I can provide a few tips to get you started. Here are the tips won from hard experience:

Tip 1. Record and digitize at the right amplitude. Web audio requires careful attention to proper signal levels at all stages of production.

Digital audio is much less forgiving of distortion than analog, so it is critically important that the signal not be pushed to clipping at any point. On the other hand, it is equally important to maintain as high a signal to noise ratio as possible for best final product after converting to a Web-friendly format. Judicious application of a compressor-limiter can guard against distortion while maintaining the overall high signal level appropriate for the Web. (Incidentally, the amplitude compression alluded to here is not the same as file compression discussed below.)

Tip 2. Aim for small file size in the final product. Even with the recent advances in Internet technology, the pipe is still small. It requires a careful balance between quality and compression, and it requires some forethought on what is really necessary to get the message across. Here are some suggestions for keeping the file size as small as possible:

a. Digitize to mono rather than stereo. For most purposes the stereo effect is not worth the added file size.

b. Digitize short representative clips when possible rather than entire works.

c. Avoid using .wav or .aif files as final output; choose mpeg (.mp3) or RealAudio (.ra) or audio Quicktime (.mov) instead.

d. Set an appropriate file compression level. For MP3s a setting of 64 kilobits per second is adequate for most music on the Web. For voice narrations, a setting as low as 16 Kbps works. Some commercial Internet music sites like MP3.com often insist that uploaded files be 128 Kbps and stereo.

e. Choose a streaming file format. Although your school district may not have a dedicated streaming server, it's easily possible to create a format that allows a file to start playing before it has completely downloaded. For most purposes, this has the same effect.

Tip 3. Put all files in the same folder before you begin to build the Web page. This advice may appear simplistic, but for novices it is the number one reason that Web pages containing seemingly functional images and audio doesn't work when uploaded to the server. Put the HTML, the pictures, and the sound files all in one folder and then upload the entire folder.

Tip 4. Start with the basics. If you don't have experience in putting audio on the Web, you can learn the techniques most efficiently by starting with basic Web pages and short audio clips. You can always add more complexity later.

This article originally appeared in the Winter 2001 issue of Texas's TMEC Connections. Reprinted by permission.

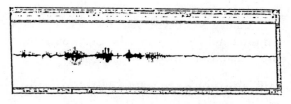

Image 1
Too hot a signal causes distortion due to clipping.

Image 2
Too low a signal makes the signal to noise ratio unacceptable

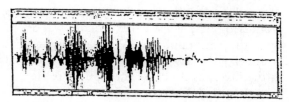

Image 3
An acceptable waveform uses 60% to 80% of an editor window's height.

Your Program's Very Own Web Site
Tobin Shucha

The World Wide Web provides a remarkable public relations opportunity. While access for creating a site is readily available and relatively inexpensive, a well-designed Web site still gives people the impression that an organization is professional and vibrant. And if you're someone who thinks they don't have to be concerned with their music program's public image, the practical uses your program can get out of having its own Web site may be even greater.

It may seem like a techno-dream to some. After all, just a little over five years ago, we were wondering why www.whatever.com was popping up at the bottom of our TV screens on every commercial. Today, however, 41.5% of households in the U.S. have Internet access; if there are school-aged children in the home, it rises to 53.5%. And 30.4% of children, and 47.9% of children ages 12–17, use the Internet at home (source: U.S. Census Bureau, August 2000). Our "customers" are online, and more are going there every year. When you consider this, along with the fact that information on a Web site is available 24 hours a day, 365 days a year, the costs of a Web site (in time and money) are a bargain compared to more traditional media.

What to put on a Web site about the music program

Don't forget that they call the Internet the information superhighway. Use it to get out information that you want students, parents, and the general public to know about the music program. Any information in your student handbook—classroom rules/expectations, performance dates, grading criteria, concert dress expectations— is the kind of information that you can put on your Web site and keep there for long periods of time. In the Waunakee School District, we have saved ourselves untold phone calls with questions about this kind of information by putting it on our Web site. While we still print up newsletters and send them home with students and through the mail, the Web site is never lost before it gets home, never tossed out with the junk mail, and is always there when people have questions.

If you have the resources to update your Web page on a regular basis, you may even want to include information about upcoming events, recent occurrences, and assignments. But remember, it's better to leave information off your Web site than to have it be outdated. If you can't keep up with updates, stick to information that can stay on your site for the long term.

In addition to these practical solutions, a Web site is also, of course, a very strong public relations tool. Unlike the print or broadcast media, you control your Web site, so you always get the coverage you want. You can post photos of your students performing or doing special projects, service activities, or interdisciplinary units. Always check your district's policy on posting student photos and how students can be identified on the Web. If you don't think there is a policy, ask an administrator! A Web page also provides the perfect opportunity to promote the successes of your program without feeling like you're "blowing your own horn." After all, people who visit your Web site are really looking for what's up with your program—let them know the positives!

Okay, there are lots of ideas ... now what? I'm very fortunate in this respect. I have an extensive district Web site already in place, partners who have already designed Web sites for our programs, and an amazing person in the building that will put our updates on the Web within hours of receiving the information. If you're in a similar situation, maintaining a Web site is just a matter of visiting all the pages periodically to check for broken links and information that needs to be updated, taking lots of pictures, and giving the updates to your Web person.

Another situation may be that your district is willing to give your program space on its server (a place to put your Web site), but you have to build and maintain it yourself. In this case, taking a course on Web site design will really help. Often, you get a great start on building your Web site while taking the course. One place to find courses online (designed for teachers) on Web site design as well as many other technology areas is Connected University at www.cu.classroom.com.

If you can't get server space from your district, don't know how to build a Web site, or just want to get your information out on the Web without a lot of hassle, there are free Web hosting sites available. One that is designed specifically for teachers is www.teacherweb.com. At this site, you can build a simple, but effective, Web site without having to know anything about Web design. You simply visit the site, build a page by typing in what you want, and assign a password that will be needed to update the information. You can't put your pictures on this kind of Web site, though, and it's more difficult for people to remember the address if it's not linked to a district Web site.

However you decide to implement your Web site, make sure to advertise it! Put your Web address in concert programs and parent newsletters, try to mention it at parent/teacher conferences, and make sure your students know how to get there.

The World Wide Web is a powerful tool, and one that you can use to help your program succeed. If you don't already have a Web site, there are many ways to get started. The most important step is the first one—take that step and get your program's Web site going!

This article first appeared in the December 2001 issue of the Wisconsin School Musician. *Reprinted by permission.*

Home Practice Online! Creating and Implementing an Interactive Web Page for Your Students

Scott Watson

The Internet opens up all sorts of possibilities for music instruction outside of the confines of a rehearsal period or the space confines of a room in the school building. At present, only a minority of students have Internet access at home, but this is quickly changing. The possibility of 40 to 50 percent of our students being online in the next year or two is very real and the music educator who uses this resource will tap into a unique teaching and motivational tool.

In the Parkland School District in Allentown, PA—about an hour north of Philadelphia—I teach elementary instrumental music. Like many communities at the intersection of town and country, our district population has grown dramatically in the past 10 years, making classrooms more crowded. At the same time, due to the increase in mandated and elective programs and services, time during the school day has become a heavily contested-for commodity. I meet with my fourth and fifth grade band students once a week in small group lessons, but not in full band rehearsals until a few weeks before a concert. This increasingly all-too-familiar environment necessitated the creation of "Home Practice Online!", a Web site that allows students to practice at home via the Internet in a virtual, electronic rehearsal setting. Students can set up their band music near their computer, log on to the site, and perform along to midi realizations of their concert music as it is played back through their web browser. You can visit "Home Practice Online!" at: www.enter.net/~ascott/parkland.html.

The site cannot replace face to face instruction; in fact, students are not ready to practice online until they can reasonably perform their part in a song that has been introduced in school lessons. Some students do visit the site to hear what a song sounds like with all the parts. Primarily, "Home Practice Online!" motivates members of this "tech generation" to practice, while simulating the ensemble experience and thus better preparing them for in-school rehearsals.

What has been the reaction from the students who use the site and their parents? An e-mail link at the site enables me to receive their feedback. One 6th grade flutist told me, "Thanks to this site, I now know exactly where I fit in. It is a great help!" A parent of a 5th grade clarinetist wrote, "Caitlin's enthusiasm has grown even more when practicing. What a unique way to motivate these youngsters!" Some students use the e-mail link to ask me about an instrument fingering or other item necessary for their home practice. Since I teach in three buildings and only see each student once a week, I'm glad for the opportunity to help them out online after our in-school lesson.

Following a very successful initial meeting of our 4th grade full band last spring, I conducted an informal poll. When asked how many had already practiced their concert selections online, one third of the band raised their hands. A nucleus of the ensemble which had already been rehearsing online was used to hearing and playing with the other parts sounded by various sections of the band.

Although I teach elementary band, a home practice site might feature general music songs for student review or concert music accompaniments with which chorus members can rehearse, or even chord changes with which your jazz band soloists can jam. Only your imagination limits you. Why not post field show music to the site for the color guard and drum line, etc? Might it help your singers who audition for district chorus to have their audition music online for drilling at home?

Although the process of creating a Web site with multimedia involves several facets and is not for computer beginners, it can be summarized quite simply. For matters of brevity, this article assumes familiarity with the Internet, word processing, and basic sequencing skills. For those who want to investigate further, I've posted an outline of this entire process, with many helpful links to get you going, on the web at: www.enter.net/~ ascott/NSMIT/outline.html.

Amateur Web pages are usually created using either Web page authoring software such as Claris Home Page or Microsoft Front Page, or by creating a document as you normally would with most word processing and presentation applications (such as Microsoft Word or Power Point) and saving the document as an HTML file. HTML— or Hypertex Markup Language—is the language behind every Web page. Programs such as Front Page or Word let you create Web pages without having to see or understand HTML. However, despite it technical sounding name, HTML is not all that difficult to work with directly. If all you had was a simple text editor, you could still probably create your first simple Web page by typing the actual HTML code after just a few hours with an entry-level book such as *HTML for Dummies*.

A "Home Practice" site should be organized around its central content: electronic realizations of concert music, etc. I use MIDI sequences of the music I want to post since they take up less memory than digital audio files and because I have the flexibility of sequencing anything I need (rather than hoping that a recording exists). With all software sequencers—such as Performer (MOTU), Vision (Opcode) or Master Tracks Pro (G-Vox)—a song can be input and then saved as a Standard MIDI File (SMF). Remember to include a one-measure "count off" to help your students anticipate the first beat of the song. I use a wood block or snare sound for this. Sequences need to be saved as SMFs, with the file name extension .mid added, in order to be recognized by a web page's HTML code. Another option is to create a Quick Time movie of a MIDI File, giving it the extension .mov. To do this, launch Movie Player—a part of the Quick Time suite—and import your MIDI file. The file is converted to a movie with no picture, just audio. Either way, the .mid or .mov file is regarded as an embedded object which can be played back in a browser when the user clicks on whatever you designate as the hypertext link to

the MIDI file of the song (say the song's title). Here's the only catch: the student's browser must have a plug-in to play back MIDI files such as Crescendo (available free from www.liveupdate .com) or Quick Time. This isn't much of a problem since most newer systems and newer versions of browser software come equipped with these multimedia helpers.

Although your Web page will be viewed as a whole on the web, it really consists of one main HTML document and a bunch of associated files: graphic images, MIDI files, other linked pages, and possibly more. After a Web page, including all its related files, is prepared, everything needs to be uploaded to the server (space on the hard drive of a fairly serious computer) which will host the site. The easiest way to go is to give all these files to your school's technology paraprofessional and have him or her upload your page for you. However, especially if you'll be making frequent updates, you can do it yourself with an Internet connection and an FTP (file transfer protocol) program.

One such program, Fetch, is available from Dartmouth University for free download to educators (www.dartmouth.edu/pages/softdev/ fetch.html). The program asks you to input the electronic address of the server to which you'll be sending everything (usually something like ftp.ivyleague.edu) and a password (given you by your Internet service provider when you receive permission to upload), then send the files electronically. In moments everything is on the Web for all your students to access!

One final point needs to be made: although most publishers are happy to give you permission to make .mid file arrangements of their music for a nonprofit, educational Web site, you need to ask and receive a release first! I keep this process simple by using a form letter I've created. I fill in the pertinent information (song title, composer, copyright date, etc.) and fax it to the publisher. I usually get an answer in days and so far no one has denied permission.

This article originally appeared in the March 2000 issue of Pennsylvania's PMEA News. *Reprinted by permission.*

Section 4

# Technology and Web Resources

Section 4

Technology and Web Resources

Good Internet Music Resources? Music Resources for Elementary, Middle, High School, and College
Kerri Clark

Does the Internet have good music resources? Are these resources reliable? Can you use these resources in your classroom? Yes, the Internet does in fact have some good music Web sites. By researching many music sites such as MENC, J. W. Pepper and Alfred Publications (over 170 sites were reviewed), I found some resourceful and educational links. These links can be used within your classroom as well as a reference for the music educator.

The following links are grouped into 4 categories. These categories include elementary school, middle school, high school, and college/university. Some links will be duplicated within the categories due to information applicable to multiple age-groups.

Elementary School
Start the Music Strategies
www.menc.org/guides/startmusic/contents.htm
Easy-to-use strategies on understanding the basic and integral part of a child's education. "And just as music has to be understood as integral to learning, so must it be considered as integral to life, as an activity in which every child can participate fully. It is truly time to start the music."

DataDragon
http://datadragon.com/education/
"Come and explore some parts of music with the DataDragon online tutorials and guides." Some of the items include—learn and hear about different instruments, learn to read music, and this day in music history.

The Guide to Charlie Horse Music Pizza—the Shari Lewis educational series
www.menc.org/guides/charguid/charopen.html
Teaching activities that accompany Shari Lewis' PBS show, *The Charlie Horse Music Pizza*. "Children's achievement can be amplified by working with music in daycare, at school, or at home. The lesson plans in this guide are designed to suggest strategies for helping children in this way."

Jammin' 5 a Day Songs from Dole Food Company and MENC
www.menc.org/guides/dole/index.html
"This Teacher's Guide is a creative and innovative way to incorporate the songs (developed by Dole) into your classroom music curriculum while supporting aspects of our science, nutrition, and physical education curricula as well."

Celebrate Dr. Martin Luther King Jr.'s Legacy with JAZZ
www.menc.org/guides/mlk/mlk.html
"A lesson with interdisciplinary connections for middle-level music students"

Duke Ellington: Celebrating 100 Years of the Man and His Music
www.dellington.org/
Interactive lessons on Duke Ellington. Some links that are included on this site are timelinks, resources, student gallery, etc.

Get America Singing ... Again! In the Classroom
www.menc.org/information/prek12/again.html
"This campaign has two major objectives: the

first of which is to establish a common song repertoire that 'Americans, of all ages, know and can sing.' … The campaign's second objective is to promote community singing." The songs chosen for *Get America Singing … Again!* "are appropriate for home, community, and classroom."

The New York Philharmonic Kidzone!
www.nyphilkids.org/

An interactive children's Web site. This site has information regarding composers, musical instruments, news and much more.

Middle School

Duke Ellington: Celebrating 100 Years of the Man and His Music
www.dellington.org/

Interactive lessons on Duke Ellington. Some links that are included on this site are timelinks, resources, student gallery, etc.

Jazz: A Film by Ken Bums—General Motors Music Study Guide for Grades 5–8
www.pbs.org/jazz/classroom/

"Jazzy lessons and activities for K–12 cats. The resources offered here are designed to help you use the PBS JAZZ video series and companion Web site in music, social studies, math, and language arts classes."

The 2001 Music in Our Schools Month and World's Largest Concert Teacher's Guide
www.menc.org/guides/wlc/wlccover.htm

"Our theme this year, 'Music … Pass It On!' offers some insight in to the traditions and importance of passing music from one generation and one culture to the next."

DataDragon
http://datadragon.com/education/

"Come and explore some parts of music with the DataDragon online tutorials and guides." Some of the items include—learn and hear about different instruments, learn to read music, and this day in music history.

The Guide to Teaching with Popular Music
www.menc.org/guides/nsync/open.htm

"Teaching with popular music becomes part of a broad-based effort to include more of America's children in a balanced, sequential music education program."

Opera: All of Music and More
www.menc.org/guides/opera/opfront.html

"Use opera to teach music and extend into language arts and social studies. Developed by MENC with the generous support of Texaco Inc., New York Philharmonic LIVE! The 11 lessons and 16 reproducible master sheets contained in the publication cover the rich interdisciplinary field of opera in a way designed to help students come to know and love opera and to work toward achievement in the National Standards for Music Education."

Kyle's Virtual Guitar Lessons
www.supersonic.net/guitar/

"This site is designed to be a resource for beginning and frustrated guitar players who are looking to improve their guitar playing skills."

Celebrate Dr. Martin Luther King Jr.'s Legacy with JAZZ
www.menc.org/guides/mlk/mlk.html

"A lesson with interdisciplinary connections for middle level music students"

Get America Singing … Again! In the Classroom
www.menc.org/information/prek12/again.html

"This campaign has two major objectives: the first of which is to establish a common song repertoire that 'Americans, of all ages, know and can sing.' … The campaign's second objective is to promote community singing." The songs chosen for *Get America Singing … Again!* "are appropriate for home, community, and classroom."

High School

Careers in Music—an MENC brochure
www.menc.org/industry/job/careers/careers.html

"If you are thinking about a career in music, this brochure will provide you with valuable information. It lists salary ranges, personal qualifications, required knowledge and skills, recommended precollege training, and recommended college education and other training for a wide array of music jobs."

Why Teach, Why Music, Why Me?
http://www.menc.org/guides/whyteach/whymusic.html

"Today more young people than ever want a career in which they can merge artistic talent, academic preparation, and idealism in satisfying and meaningful ways. Teaching can provide that career."

The Guide to Guitar in the Classroom

www.menc.org/music_classes/guitar/intro.html

"This guide is designed to provide teachers with the information they need to launch a successful guitar program. It is made up of four elements: Guitar: A Course for All Reasons; A Strategy for Teaching; The Guitar: Past, Present, and Future; and a list of resources."

The Guide to Teaching with Popular Music

www.menc.org/guides/nsync/open.htm

"Teaching with popular music becomes part of a broad based effort to include more of America's children in a balanced, sequential music education program."

Opera: All of Music and More

www.menc.org/guides/opera/opfront.html

"Use opera to teach music and extend into language arts and social studies. Developed by MENC with the generous support of Texaco Inc., New York Philharmonic LIVE! The 11 lessons and 16 reproducible master sheets contained in the publication cover the rich interdisciplinary field of opera in a way designed to help students come to know and love opera and to work toward achievement in the National Standards for Music Education."

Kyle's Virtual Guitar Lessons

www.supersonic.net/guitar/

"This site is designed to be a resource for beginning and frustrated guitar players who are looking to improve their guitar playing skills."

Celebrate Dr. Martin Luther King Jr.'s Legacy with JAZZ

www.menc.org/guides/mlk/mlk.html

"A lesson with interdisciplinary connections for middle-level music students"

Duke Ellington: Celebrating 100 Years of the Man and His Music

www.dellington.org/

Interactive lessons on Duke Ellington. Some links that are included on this site are timelinks, resources, student gallery, etc.

College/University

The Music Code of Ethics

www.menc.org/publication/books/ethics.html

"An agreement defining the jurisdictions of music educators and professional musicians."

Opportunity-to-Learn Standards for Music Instruction, Grades Pre K–12

www.menc.org/publication/books/otl.html

"While the opportunity-to-learn standards focus on the learning environment necessary to teach music, it is important to note that the ultimate objective of all standards, all school curriculums, and all school personnel is to help students to gain the broad skills and knowledge that will enable them to function effectively as adults and contribute to society in today's world and tomorrow's."

Careers in Music—an MENC brochure

www.menc.org/industry/job/careers/careers.html

"If you are thinking about a career in music, this brochure will provide you with valuable information. It lists salary ranges, personal qualifications, required knowledge and skills, recommended precollege training, and recommended college education and other training for a wide array of music jobs."

Why Teach, Why Music, Why Me?

www.menc.org/guides/whyteach/whymusic.html

"Today more young people than ever want to career in which they can merge artistic talent, academic preparation, and idealism in satisfying and meaningful ways. Teaching can provide that career."

Music Educators Journal

www.menc.org/publication/articles/mejindex.html

Searchable index that is available via microfilm and/or electronic databases from: Bell & Howell Information and Learning, EBSCO, Gale Group and The H. W. Wilson Company.

A Career Guide to Music Education by Barbara Payne

www.menc.org/industry/job/caropen.html

"Need to know where to look for a job? What to wear to an interview? Want to know what they might ask you at an interview? This site is for you!"

The United States Copyright Law: A Guide for Music Educators

www.menc.org/information/copyright/copyr.html

"It is a law that must be understood by music educators, both to improve their teaching and to protect themselves and their schools from incurring liability or subjecting themselves to the possibility of being sued."

From one organization to another there are tons of musical Web sites that are out there for your finding. There are sites geared towards elementary school, middle school, high school and the college/university level, plus there are sites that are applicable to all age groups. The sites presented were just a few sites that I came across as being helpful and resourceful for the student as well as the music educator. Enjoy!

This article originally appeared in the March 2002 issue of Kentucky's Bluegrass Music News. *Reprinted by permission.*

Secondary General Music on the Web
David Fodor

This issue, we will explore a few of the resources available to you on the Web for building nonperformance curriculum, developing standards-based assessment, and promoting advocacy for SGM classes in your school. So fire up your computers and go online with your favorite Web browser as you read along!

If you type the words "secondary general music" into your favorite search engine, most of the sites you find will be college and university pages designed by professors for their education methods courses. These can actually be good jumping off points in your search for help if the sites have hyperlinks to other pages. If you are new to teaching secondary general music, these higher education pages may even inspire you to go take a class next summer (and don't forget to include that training in your Illinois recertification plan!). For example, one course page that grabbed my attention was designed by Dr. Carlos Rodriguez for his course at the University of Iowa. You can find it at: http://www. uiowa.edu/~genmusic/ 142syllabus.html.

Advocacy/State Policy
There are many, many sites on the Web for obtaining articles and research on the value of a music education. The first site below is one example of a state-level policy regarding the importance of secondary music education for all students.
- The Wisconsin Music Educators have posted a statement of justification and guidelines for the implementation of nonperformance courses in an effort to give all students the opportunity to explore music. This well-defined position can be found at: http://www. wmea.com/about/ sec_pos.html.
- Music is ... and the value of music education" is a Web site full of useful articles describing a wide variety of positive aspects of a music education: http://pionet.net/~hub7/.
- The Children's Music Workshop Web site lists articles promoting the values of a music education on its music advocacy page located at http://www.geocities.com/Athens/2405/feature.html.
- The American Music Conference site presents a wide variety of music advocacy information at: http://www.amc-music.com/.

Online Curricular Resources
The sites below cover a variety of curriculum issues from research and units of study to specific methodologies and methods

- *General Music Today* is a journal which may help in your search for important studies in the field, ideas for curriculum, or just thinking about new ideas. The address below is an index of volumes 1 through 13 of the journal, compiled on the MENC Web site: http://www.menc. org/ publication/articles/gmtindex.html.
- D. Harris has compiled a number of resources for SGM on his Web site for a methods class at the University of Saskatchewan. Topics here include the elements of music and musical styles, processes in music and the arts listening, composing roles in music, issues in music/the arts, music education in a global Community, and theory and analysis. http://www.usask. ca/education/coursework/ edmus340/ materials/ressecgen.htm.
- This online teaching center for elementary general music teachers will offer some useful tools for secondary teachers as well: http://www.general music.org/.
- Teachers who want to explore the Kodály method can access information at http://www.kodaly-inst.hu/kodaly/iks.htm.
- Teachers who want to explore the Orff method can access information at http://www.aosa. org/AOSA.shtml.

Teaching With Technology
No other educational tool has had as much impact on our teaching this generation than the advancement of technology. Here are but a few Web pages that you should know about in your quest to integrate technology into your curriculums.

- Go to TI-ME (Technology Institute for Music Educators) for online help with technology issues http://www.ti-me.org/ti-me/default.html.
- A fun site to visit for help with technology issues is run by professors Peter Webster of Northwestern University and David Williams of Illinois State University: http://www.music.org/sqk_blat/.
- Dr. Sam Reese at the University of Illinois has created a Web site called "Music Teachers & Technology" which offers a "Systems Approach" to the application of technology in your classroom: http://www-camil.music.uiuc.edu/tbmi/.
- Another site close to home is the IMEA Composition Contest Page, where you can find out more about how to get your students involved in putting their works out into the public eye: http://www.ilmea.org/page20.htm.
- If you are looking for another way for your students to interact with others in their quest for musical composition experience, check out this opportunity created by professor Maud Hickey at Northwestern University. "Micnet" is a collaborative space on the Web where students can share original MIDI compositions and send comments to other student composers. They can even download each other's files for editing and revisions, and then upload them for further comments. Schools may join the musical collaboratory project for free by going to: http://collaboratory.nunet.net/micnet/.

Curriculum Design and the Standards

Illinois school teachers are working to align their curriculums with the Illinois learning standards. Listed below are several excellent models of curriculum design systems and links to our own Illinois State Learning Standards:

- One very popular curriculum design system for use across all subjects is called "Understanding by Design." Visit this site to learn more about how to build courses, units of study, and activities by beginning first with what many teachers think about last in their planning—assessment and linking to the standards: http://ubd.ascd.org/.
- ALPS (Active Learning Practice for Schools) is an electronic community dedicated to the improvement and advancement of educational instruction and practice. Our mission is to create an online collaboration between teachers and administrators from around the world with educational researchers, professors, and curriculum designers at Harvard's Graduate School of Education and Project Zero: http://learnweb.harvard.edu/alps/.
- Need the newest information on the Illinois Learning Standards? Go here for the latest word on state-mandated standards information: http://www.isbe.state.il.us/ils/.

I hope these sites are helpful to you. If you are like me, you probably found twice as many interesting sites while you visited these examples, so put down the magazine now and head back to the Web—unless, of course, you'd rather eat dinner …

This article originally appeared in the Winter 2000 issue of the Illinois Music Educator. *Reprinted by permission.*

Sites for Sore Eyes (and Ears)
John Haughey

Since the inception of computers, the marriage of music and computer technology has been a natural one. Computers and music have at their core a fundamental reliance on mathematics. Even the earliest computers made use of music playing and composing programs.

Of course, nowadays music is old hat on computers—so much so that I don't believe we really need many more inservice or convention clinics on the subject. Those of us who are inclined to use computers in our teaching have probably already done so.

The Internet has become a great resource for music educators. People are coming up with great concepts for the distribution and study of music. I thought you might find useful some of the Web sites I have run across:

The Choral Public Domain Library (CPDL) www.cpdl.org is probably the most beneficial place for choral directors. It contains over 3,200 choral scores including great works from great composers. All the music is in the public domain and hence can be copied, distributed, and performed without any royalty fees. A search for Bach retrieves 98 scores; one for Bruckner, 24 scores; one for Renaissance, 1,442 scores. The scores are downloadable in one or more of these formats: Adobe PDF, Finale, Encore, MIDI, and sometimes Sibelius. The editions I have used or perused are just as good if not better than the ones being sold for

$1.50–$5.00 by publishers. This is a great resource! It is such a good idea that I decided to donate money to the organization in hopes that it will continue its efforts. There are also a lot of good links to other choral sites on their Web page.

Java language is a tool Web publishers use to install a small program on your computer. Many of the programs written in Java are similar in size and capability to programs that ran on computers 8 to 10 years ago. The advantage is that they are free, run temporarily from the Web, and are gone when you quit the Net. Also, the programs can be run by any computer connected to the Internet

http://www.teoria.com has a Java-based music theory site which explains intervals, chords, and scales.

http://web1.hamilton.edu/javamusic/default.html is a Java-based site which offers drills in note reading, intervals, chords, scales, key signatures, and other stuff.

http://www.good-ear.com has ear-training exercises in which a pitch or interval is played and you must chose the button which indicates the type of interval it is. It also has modules for chords, scales, jazz chords, cadences, note locations, and perfect pitch.

http://www.chordwizard.com/theorvintro.html offers Fundamentals of Music and Multimedia Music Theory. This site gives some explanation of the acoustical properties of sound.

http://www.musical-theory.com, a non-Java-based site which offers a straightforward explanation of musical concepts in a text-and-image format.

All of the above sites will work for any of our students at home who have a computer connected to the Internet. I think I'll give some assignments to kids who are sick at home.

This article first appeared in the April 2002 issue of *Montana's* Cadenza. *Reprinted by permission.*

An Indispensable Guide to WWW Resources
Michael Ross, Karen Frink, and Chris Gleason

In this month's column, the WMEA State Band, Orchestra, and Choral Chairs have combined to bring you a list of sites you might find helpful for information, repertoire ideas, and literature purchase. Try them, find others, go World Wide Web crazy! And, don't forget to check out the wmea.com Web site for even more (new) links!

National Organizations
www.menc.org
  The Web site of the largest music organization in the world: MENC.
www.astaweb.com
  The official Web site of ASTA WITH NSOA provides string and orchestra teachers the opportunity to order educational publications, including the *String Orchestra Super List* and other graded repertoire lists.
www.nationalbandassoc.org
  National Band Association
www.asbda.com
  American School Band Directors Association
www.iaje.org
  International Association of Jazz Educators

www.afn.org/~encore/
  Association of Concert Bands
www.cbdna.org/
  College Band Directors National Association
www.acdaonline.org
  American Choral Directors Association
www.nats.org
  National Association of Teachers of Singing

Music Publishers
www.schirmer.com
  G. Schirmer, Inc.
www.boosey.com
  Boosey & Hawkes; home to the catalogues of a vast number of composers, including Bernstein, Rachmaninoff, Vaughn Williams, Copland, and Bartok.
www.earthsongsmus.com
  Earthsong; publisher of choral music and recordings from around the world.
www.hildegard.com
  Publisher of the (choral) music of Hildegard von Bingen and others.
www.musicrussica.com
  Publisher of Russian choral music. Excellent editions.
http://TrebleClefPress.com
  Publisher of choral music for sopranos and

altos, with an emphasis on women composers.

www.arts.unco.edu/uncjazz/jazzpress.html
UNC Jazz Press catalog; excellent (and challenging) vocal jazz and jazz ensemble arrangements.

Repertoire Ideas and Catalogs

www.musicanet.org
International database of choral repertoire.

www.choralnet.org
Extensive database of choral repertoire, information, connections. Includes links to publishers, vast lists of repertoire in various categories and searchable databases. Visit this site often!

www.net4music.com
Net4music digital sheet music.

http://choral.carleton.edu
A searchable database and list of multicultural literature.

www.lucksmusic.net
Luck's Music Library, located in Michigan, publishes 5 orchestra music catalogs annually, standard orchestra literature, educational orchestra music, conductor scores, music from movies and Broadway, and solo and ensemble literature. The contents of all 5 of these catalogs are now available at their Web site, along with new publications information and the opportunity to order online

www.123sheetmusic.net
Although this Web site features a huge collection of sheet music for a variety of instruments and in a wide range of styles, it is not specifically geared to music educators.

www.jwpepper.com
The Web site for J.W Pepper not only provides the Internet user with a complete music catalog, but it is possible to view the first page of any score available. Teachers may also view music contest lists from other states and organizations for programming ideas.

www.shattingermusic.com
Shattinger Music Online

www.sharmusic.com
SHAR Products Company in Michigan. Their large selection of solo and ensemble music for strings is available for browsing and buying online.

www.markcustom.com/
Mark Records site allows you to peruse their vast CD database of recordings. A good place to start for literature ideas.

This article first appeared in the December 2001 issue of the Wisconsin School Musician. *Reprinted by permission*

Useful Web Sites for the Elementary Music Educator
Judith Willink

I admit it. Kicking and screaming, I have been dragged into the era of technology! But now that I'm here, I'm realizing it is not so bad! Any music educator, myself included, who graduated from an institution of higher learning in the 70s did not grow up with computers as students do today. (I'm looking for some sympathy here.) We have been mostly self-taught, picking up what knowledge we could from friends and an occasional short-lived computer class. One of these classes led me to discover the wealth of information available on the Internet that pertains to my general music teaching.

As we all know, once you are into the Web, hours can be lost meandering here and there! And the information seems endless! For example, on just one search engine—Web Crawler—there are 6,087,885 listings under the heading of "elementary music education." Where does one begin?

Many of these sites are posted because somewhere in the text of the document the word "music" appears. Some of the sites are advertising for colleges, universities, and other centers of learning that grant music degrees. You have to be very specific with the subject you are searching for. And not everyone who creates a Web site or submits material has credentials or any particular expertise in the area they represent. Some Web sites aren't worth the time and effort of clicking them up! And it does take time to sift through these. But some sites are great sources for curriculum and instruction ideas, lesson plans, and catalogs for classroom materials.

Here is my compilation of some favorite Web sites, listed by category. I hope these sites will prove useful to other elementary general music teachers. I need to acknowledge two technology gurus who recommended several of their favorite Web sites for this list. My thanks to Nancy Rasmussen, our WMEA president-elect, and to Anne Sheridan, fellow elementary music teacher and "techno-wizard" in the Eau Claire School District, for their assistance and suggestions.

Music Literacy

- **www.lessonplanspage.com**—lesson plans for music and other subjects, categorized by grade level, Pre-K through high school. Some plans cover such areas as composition, dance and movement, instruments, music components, music history, styles, singing, and connections to other curricular areas. A great, extensive resource!!
- **www.teachnet.com/lesson/music/general/index.html**
- **www.musicnotes.net**
- **www.musiceducationmadness.com**—a gathering place for music educators, sharing lesson plans and ideas.
- **www.geocities.com**—click on "music"—many links to music education subjects such as composers and music literature.e.

Composers

- **www.gmn.com/composers**—hundreds of biographies!!
- **www.home.earthlink.net/~kgann/women.html** —list of women composers
- **www.composers.net**—composers page

Styles, Instruments

- **www.allmusic.com**—comprehensive site dealing with various styles of music and artists, past and present.
- **www.artforkids.about.com**

- **www.musicians.about.com**
- **www.musicforkids.com**
- **www.playmusic.org**
- **www.pbskids.org/africa**—samples of thumb piano music

Retail

- **www.netstoreusa.com**—a site for searching for sheet music, old and new; music posters, motivational materials, etc.
- **www.larkinam.com**—Lark in the Morning company, a musician's service that specializes in hard-to-find musical instruments and instructional materials: books, recordings, videos. A great place to look for ethnic instruments for multicultural music curriculums.

And, of course, don't forget to frequently visit useful music education association Web sites such as **www.menc.org** and **www.wmea.com**.

The listing here is merely the tip of the iceberg. The Internet truly places the world at your fingertips. I encourage you to take some time and explore subject areas through the various search engines available.

This article originally appeared in the December 2001 issue of the Wisconsin School Musician. *Reprinted by permission.*

Section 5

Computer Technology: Hardware and Software

 Section 5

Computer Technology: Hardware and Software

Technology in the Classroom: Reviewing MiBAC Music Lessons and Alfred's Essentials of Music Theory
Jeff Hamilton

This article will offer suggestions for computer-aided music theory instruction in the classroom, lab, or home.

Having used Music Lessons I since 1994, I can testify that it is fun for the kids and easy for teachers, without having to rely on cartoon characters or other gimmicks to keep interest high. Music Lessons I and II are available for both Macintosh and Windows platforms. The software is by John Ellinger, senior lecturer in music, Carlton College in Northfield, Minnesota. With 25 years experience teaching guitar and lute, his wife Helen stated that John designed the first music computer lab for the college.

Affordable at $120 for Music Lessons I Fundamentals ($150 for Mac) and $150 for Music Lessons II Chords and Harmony, they offer a solid music theory program for instructing any student ready for note reading, with or without the addition of a MIDI keyboard. With 11 drills in each program and a comprehensive help system, this user-friendly software can help a student master the core music concepts.

Music Lessons I covers rhythm and time signatures, major and minor scales, modes, jazz scales, intervals, note and rest durations, along with ear training in intervals, scales, and modes. With Music Lessons I, a student will further develop the skills of visual recognition, written notation, playing skills, and ear training. The six main drills—triads, triads ear training, seventh chords, seventh chords ear training, and roman numerals allow for hundreds of exercises.

Teachers can relive their college theory classes

practicing with secondary dominants, Neapolitan, and augmented sixth chords. Multiple skill levels and custom drills, combined with score tracking, allow an unlimited number of students to move from elementary through college level theory and ear training. For further information on Music Lessons I, "lab packs," and site licensing, contact www.mibac.com or MiBAC Music Software, P.O. Box 468, Northfield, MN 55057; Tel: (507)-645-3851; Fax: 507-645-2377.

Another self-paced software for use with beginning or advanced students is Alfred's Essentials of Music Theory. Purchased separately or in the "complete" 3-volume CD-ROM set, Essentials of Music Theory follows the book of the same name. Volume 1 covers concepts from staff and notes, through note values and sharps and flats. Vol. 2 proceeds through scales, intervals, sixteenth notes, triads, and chords. A lesson covering solfège is included midway through this volume. Volume 3 covers chord progressions, minor scales, modes, and harmony. The final unit on form concludes with a review of binary, ternary, and rondo.

Throughout 18 units, with 6 per volume, aural skills are aided by a variety of acoustic instruments playing quality music examples. Music excerpts cover several time periods and cultures. The interactive learning environment introduces a music concept with narration and eye-catching graphics while integrating ear training into each lesson. Exercises reinforce each concept as it is presented. Students may highlight vocabulary for a definition or, with one click, move to the complete glossary or term screen for definitions, spoken pronunciation, and visual examples of each term. One click of the mouse and they are returned to their lesson. Scored reviews complete each unit.

The savvy customer will opt for the Complete

Student Set of Volumes 1–3 for $60, as each volume sells separately for $30 each. The Educator Version features scorekeeping of 200 students' overall scores and individual scores for each unit and concept. Student versions allow the user to track progress but do not keep records. The educator version allows the teacher to create custom tests. You can order Alfred's Essentials of Music Theory, Volumes 1–3, directly from Alfred Publishing or from your local sheet music dealer. Lab packs and site licensing are available.

This article first appeared in the May 2001 issue of Kentucky's Bluegrass Music News. *Reprinted by permission.*

Inner Hearing
William R. Higgins

Formal ear training usually begins with melodic and rhythmic dictation. Because the study of dictation requires someone to present the material (usually played on the piano) and someone to evaluate the accuracy of the responses, there is seldom enough teacher time for this activity or any other opportunity for the student to practice this important skill. The computer provides an excellent assistant for both teaching and learning the skill of melodic/rhythmic dictation. The computer can present the material and evaluate the student's performance at the same time. Utilizing the computer in a private setting also avoids the trauma of taking dictation in a class setting where peer pressure is often detrimental to learning.

Inner Hearing
By Scott McCormick
Published by Musical Hearing
Phone (508) 643-9122
http:\\www.musicalhearing.com
E-mail: scott@musicalhearing.com
For Windows and Macintosh Computers
Cost: Unit 1—$49.95; Unit 2—$49.95

Stated purpose. (1) To provide an interactive environment for learning melodic dictation skills; (2) To present interesting and valuable musical literature for dictation; (3) To exercise the musical memory and to connect sounds with musical notation; (4) To exercise and develop the process of *inner hearing*: the imagination of sounds which is the foundation of all musical activities.

Hardware required. The PC version requires Windows 3.1, 95, or 98; sound card with drivers installed or MIDI output to synthesizer; and some type of sound amplification. The Mac version requires System 7.5 or higher; MIDI interface for output to synthesizer; and some type of amplification.

Contents. The software is available in two units. Unit 1 presents 130 short folk melodies. Unit 2 utilizes 100 classical melodies that are longer and more complex than those presented in Unit 1.

Documentation. This program is so easy to use that there is virtually no need for documentation however, there is a concise and easy to follow online help menu.

Content. In Unit 1, pitch patterns and tone groups are based on Kodály principles. Actual melodies are used as opposed to computer generated tunes. Patterns begin with 4-note phrases and are sequenced to 4-measure phrases. Unit 2 uses melodies by classical composers and has more complex phrases including chromaticism and modulation.

Presentation. All dictation examples are presented on a single screen in single line notation in the treble clef. The student selects a level from the ten sequenced levels in the unit. In both the pitch and rhythm mode, notation is placed on the staff with the correct number of noteheads per measure but without pitch (all notes are on the second line) and without rhythm (all notes are quarter notes). The student uses the mouse and/or keyboard to change the pitch and rhythmic values of the notes to correspond to the aural example. The dictation can be further simplified by selecting (1) pitch only (the rhythm is given) or (2) rhythm only (the pitches are provided). When the student clicks on Check, incorrect responses are identified and the student is encouraged to correct mistakes. Correct responses move on to the next melody in the sequence.

Conclusions. This is an excellent program to introduce and practice the skill of melodic and rhythmic dictation as well as to develop tonal memory within a musical context. The units are usable from grades 4 through adult. Pros: The presentation is in a musical context. The program is easy to operate. The student controls all aspects of the program except sequence. Record keeping is excellent. Cons: The program does not automatically orient in key. The tonic must be requested from the menu when desired.

This article first appeared in the Winter 1999/2000 issue of Pennsylvania's PMEA News. *Reprinted by permission.*

Technology in the Music Room? Let Me Count the Ways

Beth Karchefsky

Encore! Encore! Or is it Finale? Or maybe MusicTime? Whatever program you are trying to work with, there is probably more to it than meets the eye. Here are two educators that have truly gone the extra mile when it comes to incorporating technology into their music rooms. They have begun to incorporate some of the most popular software into their classes. Plus they have come up with some unique ways of expanding its use. They have dedicated a lot of personal time to produce these results. Perhaps they may enlighten you as to some ways that you can get started or maybe add to what you already have going.

Tim Shelton teaches junior high students in Mentor, Ohio. His class load includes three levels of bands, boys chorus, and general music. Tim is always looking for new ways to motivate his students, and he is always coming up with something. Technology, in any sense, seems to be the key to his students excitement, so Tim used that to steer their energies.

Over a period of 5 or 6 years, Tim acquired some equipment for his classroom. I have also tried to include how these items may have been funded.
- G3 computer (school property)
- printer (personal investment)
- mobile MIDI lab, which includes:
  - Mac 8500 (donated by Allen Bradley)
  - Yamaha PSR 520 keyboard ($500 Partners in Science)
  - amplifier ($100 used)
  - dB meter (community fund-raiser)
  - Laser Printer (donated by Allen Bradley)
  - on-board speakers (community fund-raiser)
  - zip drive (principal's technology fund)
- overhead TV (community fund-raiser)
- student keyboards (school property)

As you can see, this took some long-range planning to decide what would be needed.

He also purchased several programs to use:
- Finale—$250 (personal investment)
- MusicTime—$60 (community fund-raiser)
- Band-in-a-Box (community fund-raiser
- Sound Recorder (shareware) (community fund-raiser)
- SmartMusic (Vivace) (community fund-raiser)
- Alfred Music Theory CD-ROM—$30 (community fund-raiser)

Tim has found multiple instructional uses for his programs as well as the equipment that he has available. In band rehearsals, he uses SmartMusic for tuning. It has a linear and a Korg-type tuner that he can display on the overhead TV so everyone can observe. Any instrument can check a note, any time, from their seat. Tim uses his G3 to play CD demos for the band. He also uses Sound Recorder to record rehearsals and play them back. He has discovered a great tool for improving students' listening skills, plus it is easy to use. Tim had such good luck with it for rehearsals that he is even using the computer's assistance in performances now.

Tim also uses his programs to transpose, record, or play accompaniments for soloists in preparation for solo and ensemble contest.

Have you ever felt that your keyboard skills were not adequate enough for choral activities? Well, Tim incorporates Band-in-A-Box by playing vocal warm-ups and individual parts as well as accompaniments for his boys choir. He simply assigns a different student each day to be the "accompanist." They are in charge of starting and stopping the program as needed as well as changing tempo and key. This frees up Tim to walk through the choir and coach from within. It really allows him to learn voices and deal with vocal problems much more efficiently. Again, Sound Recorder is employed and students can e-mail 4–8 measures of the group's best rehearsal efforts to their parents at work or to a friend or relative.

In general music classes, MusicTime helps to assess students' keyboard skills. The district provides several keyboards for the students to learn and practice on. Then the big test is, can they play the song with MusicTime and a metronome in real time?

As if this isn't enough, Tim has found ways for his students to get first-hand experience with this equipment and programs. Students, during study halls and before and after school, can input the hardest parts of their band or ensemble music and transpose them or work on original compositions. He even has his band officers work on producing Web pages and word processing items like printing programs. For their winter and spring programs, each band student creates his or her program notes and cover art work for the program bulletins by using the Local Area Network. For the audience, the designs and insights of the printed programs are varied and unique.

Tim's philosophy: to provide other ways to give students feedback and perspective on their performance. "Using a computer doesn't improve tone, rhythm, etc., but it gives them another reason to do the repetitions that *do* improve performance."

Tim's perseverance over the last 5 years has truly paid off for him. The Saturdays and Sundays he used to spend mulling over computer programs and classroom strategies has more or less subsided. He now spends approximately 1/2 hour per week monitoring student work and maintain the systems.

Is there more? Tim is hoping that his involvement with the technology will in turn keep him in step with his students. He is looking into the use of AutoScore, which makes any instrument a MIDI inputter. He is also searching for more ways to use SmartMusic for tuning and accompanying.

Roger Tropman, also a junior high teacher in Mentor, has spent many personal hours developing a program that he feels has made a difference. Roger deals with approximately 270 students in grades 5 through 9. His goals have been to encourage practice, strengthen analytical skills, and improve listening skills. The program that he created for his top band allows his students to hear professional tone qualities on any instrument and play along with them. He has tried to simulate the actual music—not an easy task.

Once again, the equipment was acquired over a 4 or 5 year span.
- Mac computer (personal investment)
- printer (personal investment)
- MIDIb (personal investment)
- synthesizer (personal investment)
- mixer (personal investment)
- master CDs (grant)
- 4 student Macs (school property)
- CD burner ($2000 music boosters)
- digital source—mini disc or DAT deck
- metronomes ($20/per student, music boosters)

The software used is Mosaic, which is approximately $250, another personal purchase. Roger received a $500 grant to hire professional musicians to make recordings. These recordings were based on a scale study book that he created. The pros recorded the entire book. Roger put the CDs together so that students could use them in a variety of ways. A typical assignment might be:
Record 3 sessions per week; 15 minutes each
1. Play the unit with pro. He plays ms. 1–8, then you play back. Stop CD and talk about areas of improvement. Play again with pro.
2. Play unit with accompaniment/melody or play with no melody.
3. Choose a piece of band music and do the same process that you did with the pro.

Students were given a checklist: of things they should work on and discuss with all units: notes, rhythm, pitch, tone, etc.

Roger took the professional recordings and burned them to CDs, which were marked by rehearsal letters by track. He added accompaniments made on the synthesizer through Mosaic and also cut those to CDs. Each of the units was written using Mosaic. The first original set of exercises he wrote over one summer. The booklet evolved over the next 4 or 5 years. The seventh and eighth grade scale study book is used to prepare the students for their task in ninth grade: the use of the CDs. It was written with a variety of keys, meters, dynamics, rhythms, common intervals, arpeggios, etc. The ninth grade book, of course, was more advanced but followed the same strategy.

In his effort to create better listening skills, Roger wrote or arranged songs for the whole band that he called "Blend and Balance" songs. These tunes were often pop/choral songs that were simpler to play but that he could use to talk about—of course—blend and balance. Each rehearsal goal was to use one of these and a march arrangement to work on precision and technique. All of the arranging was done on Mosaic. He could keep these arrangements archived and adjust the instrumentation quickly as the needs of the band unfolded. For added work, he might even take an old tune and transpose it to a new key or clef. Roger had students input their parts into Mosaic, and he worked on the arrangements. He also used the program for recording and playing accompaniments for solo and ensemble contest. When needed he could also cut these to CDs.

This was a big undertaking. It required a lot of computer time and planning time during his school day as well as personal time. He puts in about 5 hours a week listening to students' tapes. He currently uses the CDs for his honors band which is approximately 50 students. The students must also put in some time: 45 minutes a week of practice using the CDs and a tape recorder. They can use the computers at school during study halls and after to school to input parts and learn the software.

Roger would like to incorporate SmartMusic which would allow students to practice with the CD and change tempos, keys, etc.

Wow! Too much to input? I am sure you will agree that there are some great ideas going here. I hope that you found something to spark your technological fire or maybe just some new teaching strategies. Our students today need to be challenged with innovative thinking. Share your ideas and get them growing!

This article first appeared in the December/January 2001 issue of Ohio's TRIAD. Reprinted by permission.

Imagination and the Future of Music Technology: Part I

David Sebald

One of the primary factors that makes music technology so exciting and attractive today is that it constantly evolves. While many traditional forms of music making have undergone little or no modification for literally centuries, music technology reinvents, redefines, and renews itself every few years. It is continually changing and upgrading, sometimes slowly, but often so radically and with such impact that the changes can cause us to re-valuate the very term "musician."

As educators, we owe it to our profession and our students to stay informed of these technological trends. Every year or so, we should take time to investigate the tools that are new and different, discern whether they seem to be fads or valuable additions to our art, and ponder the implications they might have on what and how we teach.

Recently, I think I have observed a quickening of the evolutionary process. I have found myself becoming enthusiastic at the level I first felt in the early 80s when MIDI burst on the scene and ordinary people began to use computers to make music. It's not that nothing has happened with music technology during the intervening two decades, but over the last two years, several new trends have emerged and strengthened that seem to indicate a similar time of radical and impactful change. I'd like to share some observations on these trends in this article and then, in the next installment, make some predictions of what they might mean to music education throughout the coming decade.

Software vs. Hardware

The most striking trend I have perceived recently is the shift toward software instruments and sound-enhancement modules. No, hardware synthesizers, reverbs, and recording devices have not disappeared; however, in increasing numbers they are being challenged by software counterparts that need only a generic computer to run. A good example of this challenge can be seen in Native Instruments' software recreations of classic keyboards like the Hammond B3, the Yamaha DX7, and Sequential Circuits' Prophet-5. The complete original sound libraries of the two famous synths (the DX7 and Prophet-5) have been recreated along with all of the originals' signal processing and effects controls in the German company's FM7 and Pro-53 software. The recreation of the B3 as the software B4 is even more remarkable for the fact that the original was not a synthesizer at all but rather a simple organ that used rotating tone wheels for sound generators. Information and sound samples are available on the company's Web site at http://www. nativeinstruments.de.

Recreation of a few classic keyboards is by no means the limit of software synthesis recent advance. Designing a software-only instrument frees its creator to experiment with many types of sonic controls and interfaces that would be difficult or impractical in hardware. An example is Native Instruments' Absynth, which produces organic, morphing sounds via shaping controls unlike any traditional synth. Their Reaktor even allows the end user to create his own synthesizer from software modules.

Native Instruments is not alone in the field. Other new software synthesizers include Bitheadz' Unity DS-1 (www.bitheadz.com); Koblo's Stella 9000 (www.koblo.com); Emagic's EXS24, ES1, ES2, EVD6, and EVP88 (www.emagic.de); Steinberg's Model.E, HALion, Waldorf PPG Wave, and Waldorf Attack (www.steinberg.de); Edirol's VSC DX1, HQ-QR, and HQ-QS (www.edirol.com); and Muon's Electron (www.muon-software.com). Currently, there are well over 50 software synths on the market not counting the more generic sound generating technologies like Creative Labs' popular SoundFonts.

What's the difference between hardware and software synths? Sonically, nothing, as far as I can tell. There are, however, many advantages to software:

1. The cost of the software versions is usually about 1/20th of similar hardware.
2. An entire collection of full-fledged synthesizers can be stored inside a laptop computer rather than on a rack.
3. The cost of upgrading software is miniscule compared to upgrading hardware.

Software synths are also much more readily available. Most of the examples mentioned in this article are downloadable from their company Web sites. Many can be downloaded as free, time-limited demo versions, and a few are completely free, public domain applications.

Since their appearance on the musical scene, the only major disadvantage of software instruments has been latency, the lag time between when a voice is triggered and when its sound actually emerges. It can be disconcerting for a performer to hear sound even a tenth of a second after he hits the key. Thankfully, latency has been steadily decreasing as software synth engineering improves.

Of course, if the instruments are played by a MIDI file, latency is a nonissue, but even if played live from a connected MIDI keyboard, recent software instruments with latencies of less than a hundredth of a second feel comfortable to most musicians.

Software is also challenging the sound enhancement arena. Given the right program, modern CPUs like Intel's Pentium 4 and the G4 used in Macintoshes are more than fast enough to accomplish in real time the same sweetening duties as the dedicated circuits of hardware sound processors. These enhancements include every effect imaginable: reverbs, echoes, chorus, limiters, compressors, exciters, noise reducers, equalizers, de-essers, pitch-shifters, time-stretchers, and many types of distortion. Steinberg's VST (Virtual Studio Technology) plug-in architecture, which has been adopted most widely in the music software industry, allows these effects to be attached easily to a software synthesizer or digital audio program. Other technologies like MOTU's MAS (MOTU Audio System), Digidesign's RTAS (Real Time Audio Suite), Adobe's Premiere, and Microsoft's DirectX offer similar plug-in capabilities.

Software synthesis and sound shaping have already achieved parity with their hardware predecessors and in many respects have surpassed them. The immediate results of this trend are that studios are shrinking radically in both size and cost, and music creation is becoming even more accessible to the average person. For music teachers, this means that now each individual student can have access to an entire sound production studio. A fine example of this all-in-one approach is Propellerheads' Reason. This software package, now being used by music technology classes at UTSA, North Texas, and Berklee, holds a virtual rack of realistic synthesizers, sound processors, and mixers. In its most recent incarnation it features the following devices working in concert: a subtractive synthesizer, a granular synthesizer, two samplers, a drum machine, a loop player, a pattern sequencer, reverb, delay, phaser, chorus/flanger, compressor/limiter, parametric equalizer, a full-fledged MIDI and audio sequencer, and two CDs of sampled sounds. All this for an educational lab price of under $200 per station.

Audio Quality

Another trend that recently has taken a giant leap and which holds major implications for music education is the quality and accessibility of recorded sound. Sound quality is commonly evaluated using two main measures: (1) signal to noise ratio (SNR) and (2) the number of cycles that can be recorded in a second (cps). As a reference, the signal to noise ration of the human hearing apparatus is usually stated as 120 decibels from the quietest perceivable sound to the point where sound becomes painfully loud. The common reference for the number of cycles per second of human perception is between 20 and 20,000.

Historically, sound recording began as a primitive, acoustic-only process with needles digging a groove into wax or even paper cylinders. With the advent of electronic amplification, cylinders gave way to 78 rpm lacquer platters, but these still had an SNR of only about 50 dB and a severely limited frequency range. This analog technology remained basically the same through 45 rpm and 33 rpm "hi-fidelity" stereo recording with some improvement in electronics and thus the two measures of sound quality. Technologies like audio cassette, and open-reel tape allowed people who could afford it to record their own sound, but it was expensive and did nothing to improve on the quality of recorded sound. (Formats like 8-track are best forgotten.)

A major revolution in audio occurred in 1982 when the first digital recordings began to hit the market as audio CDs. Sampling at twice the upper limit of human hearing with a 16-bit signal accuracy, CD technology could produce a stereo signal with SNR of 96 dB—considered at the time to be virtually noiseless—and a frequency range that exceeded human hearing. Of course the process, based on the new laser technology and massive data storage, was too expensive for home recordists in the first decades of its existence.

Within the last few years, however, the exponential growth in data storage technology and processor speeds has made CD-quality recording mundane and has made it possible to surpass that level in many ways. With hard drives exceeding 100 GB and DVDs in the gigabyte range, the 44,100 sample per second rate of CDs has been doubled, and in some instances, doubled again to allow the possibility of recording at 192,000 samples per second. Since this sampling rate allows recording and playback of frequencies far beyond the range of human hearing, the question is, does it make any perceptible difference? The question may be debatable, but many people feel that it really does help in localization of sound source and elimination of those audible sideband frequencies that "muddy" sound reproduction. It really does sound more pristine. More importantly, the new storage technologies also allow 24-bit sample accuracy, which moves the signal to noise ratio much closer to the limit of human hearing—in other words, truly, not virtually, noiseless recording.

Pristine, noiseless sound is only one potential benefit of many. Another path that these increases in storage and speed have opened is that of multiple channel recording. Stereo has been the norm in home audio for over half a century and, because humans have, after all, only two ears, most people accepted left and right channels as all that were needed. But realistically, in the concert hall and in recently built theaters, sound comes from all directions. To emulate that sensation, 5.1 surround sound has become the norm for DVD home theaters and even some extended audio CDs. Major music sequencer manufacturers like Emagic, Steinberg, Cakewalk, and Mark of the Unicorn are upgrading their products to accommodate this format.

While the high end of recording technology seeks ever-expanding horizons, the mid level—actually the high end of a few years ago—has now become accessible to anyone with a computer. One of the audio industry's most respected developers, Digidesign, makes its 8-channel digital recording software available for free download on their Web site (www.digidesign.com) as ProTools Free.

Like recording software, the cost of stand-alone digital audio hardware like Roland's 24-track VS-2480 have dropped to the point that a high school student can afford one, while their quality and reliability have made them a suitable alternative to the $100,000 studio electronics of a decade ago.

What does this growth in recording mean for music education? As with the spread of cheap, high-quality, music creation tools, the wide diffusion of affordable audio technologies offers exciting new possibilities for the exploration of music. In the next article in this series, I'll make some predictions about why I think these possibilities are changing how we will define the term musician; how, with the application of a little imagination, we can take advantage of the possibilities for our students; and what aspects of our profession will always remain immutably secure.

This article first appeared in the Fall 2002 issue of Texas's TMEC Connections. *Reprinted by permission.*

Imagination and the Future of Music Technology: Part II
David Sebald

In Part I of this article (TMEC Connections, Fall 2002), I detailed some of the recent technological trends that seem to be reinvigorating the world of music as the new century dawns. These trends include: (1) improvement and proliferation of software-only instruments and sound enhancement modules, and (2) recent leaps in digital audio quality, accessibility, and flexibility.

New Musical Media
These advances are not the only trends that music technology is exhibiting today: recent technological innovations are also changing the very way people interact with music at every level. The previous article touched on the growth of multichannel formats like 5.1 surround sound. With the advent of home theater audio systems, this format is becoming so popular that it is possible to foresee a time when stereo will become superceded by this new standard. The spatial dimension that surround adds to music makes it more realistic and more exciting to listen to.

A similar format development is the spreading use of personal music devices. Walkman-type CD players were introduced over a decade ago and rapidly became popular because of their ability to provide high-quality music reproduction to a single listener in nearly any location without disturbing others. More recently, this technology has been complemented by the wide distribution of mini-CD and MP3 players. These devices provide even more compact size; the ruggedness to be used in more active environments like walking, jogging, or other exercising, and most importantly, the ability to both record and playback music. They also provide immense storage capacity. Within the last year it has become possible to store over a thousand typical songs on a single MP3 player. Personal CD players have kept pace mainly by dropping to approximately one-tenth of their original price and by incorporating many of the new devices' features like skip resistance and the ability to play home-recorded CDs. While surround sound and personal listening devices may seem unrelated on the surface, they are in fact allied by the fact that both provide even more alternatives to the live music experience. It is futile to argue whether this trend is "good" or "bad." In the long run it is simply another aspect of social evolution that music educators can either use or try to ignore.

Better Communication

Advances in communication technology have also affected the way people interact with music. Certainly the most important innovation in music distribution in recent history was Napster, the technology that allowed unlimited—and often illegal—peer-to-peer distribution of music via the Internet. Although the RIAA was successful in eliminating Napster, that technology's short meteoric existence created an enormous appetite for music delivered online. While it may no longer be possible (or at least easy) to find a free version of copyrighted music on the Web, it is now possible to access a nearly unlimited library of music in a vast diversity of styles and a huge variety of formats over the World Wide Web. To the music educator, this is even better than Napster.

Despite Napster's demise, it's still possible for a wired user to obtain nearly any music he wants via the Web. The only difference is that the process is now a little more expensive and a lot more legal. Music sites like ishareIt (http://ishareit.com/music.html) provide MP3 downloads for a fee. For those who still want music for nothing, Internet radio sites like Live 365 (http://www.live365.com) provide immediate access to music of all styles from all over the world. Apple's free iTunes software accesses these music sites directly from any Mac user's desktop.

For many purposes—particularly for musicians and music students—there are better alternatives to audio download sites. The Classical Music Archives site (http://www.classicalarchives.com) provides immediate access to over 20,000 works from all historical periods of music. Some are in MP3 audio format, but nearly all of these works are downloadable as MIDI files, a feature that makes it possible to print them to score for study and educational manipulation. For those who want access to MIDI files of *all* styles—over 1.3 million cataloged thus far—there is http://www. musicrobot.com. Both of these sites provide basic MIDI-to-sheet-music converters. These are just two examples of similar educationally useful music sites.

Going a step beyond the sites mentioned above, the two biggest music notation software companies, Coda (http://www.codamusic.com) and Sibelius (http://www.sibelius.com), offer browser plug-in technologies dedicated to displaying accurate notation on the Web and performing it from the notation.

Many music sequencer and audio software manufacturers including Digidesign, Emagic, Euphonix, Steinberg, SADiE, TASCAM, DSP Media, MOTU,

and Waveframe have recently banded together to provide an Internet service (http://www.rocketnetwork.com) that facilitates music project collaboration in near real time from any place in the world.

New Musical Interfaces

The initiation of MIDI in 1981 was certainly one of the great innovations in the history of music. For the first time, a creative musician was not restricted to real-time performance to communicate his musical concepts. Instead, like a visual artist, he could sculpt and manipulate his work at his leisure, and when he felt the work was finished, he could submit it to public performance. However, the main shortcoming of this method of music creation was that it often omitted the real-time feel and sound of live performance.

Within the last 5 years, a new technology has emerged that may alleviate this shortcoming. This is the audio loop player, basically a sequencer interface that allows the creative musician to link together short segments of audio rather than MIDI commands. These individual segments, performed by top artists and cataloged on style-related CDs, can be manipulated in a variety of ways—speed, pitch, sub-segmentation—and then combined on several audio tracks to create the final work. Examples of this software are Sonic Foundry's Acid (for PC), BitHeadz' Phrazer (for Mac), and Ableton Live (for either platform). Literally thousands of loop CDs exist or provide content for these programs.

Of course, the question arises as to whether putting together parts of someone else's performance is really making music. Again, we would be better served to avoid the good or bad controversy (except perhaps to note the similarity between this software's function and that of an ensemble director) and instead, simply think of how this technology could be used to teach musical concepts.

Even live performance has been affected by recent technological innovation. Not long ago the interfaces (OK, "instruments") that people used to perform music were exclusively acoustic or perhaps electronically amplified acoustic, like electric guitar. Aside from the keyboard synthesizer, there were few instruments that could be considered interfaces for computer generated sounds. Within the last decade, this has changed to the point that today nearly every acoustic instrument has had a computer interfaced counterpart. These range from Yamaha's WX-5 MIDI Wind Controller and Akai's Electronic Valve Instrument to Zeta's MIDI stringed instruments and Alternate Mode's various KAT percussion controllers. They include MIDI banjos, MIDI voice trackers, and a plethora of MIDI drum sets.

Predictions

As the previous article indicated and the above additions reinforce, many exciting technological trends are currently influencing the world of music. Based on our observations of these trends, can we draw some vectors into the future and make predictions about where they will lead over the next decade? Can we pull from these predictions any implications for how our profession should prepare for the future?

We all know that predictions about technology can be notoriously inaccurate. Note a few famous technology predictions made over the last 60 years: Thomas Watson (IBM)—"I think there is a world market for maybe 5 computers," Ken Olsen (Digital Equipment Corporation)—"There is no reason why anyone would want a computer in their home," Bill Gates (Microsoft)—"640K ought to be enough for anyone." So, with this kind of record, can my predictions be any more accurate than theirs?

Well, yes, if they are broad enough and solidly based on current trends. You be the judge.

Prediction #1: Music technology will continue to advance.

Yes, the prediction is obvious, but even though we all accept the statement, few of us actually act upon it. It's so much easier to simply teach what we've been taught than it is to think about what kind of musical training will be relevant to our students' lives in the future. We continue to use pedagogical models that were created to teach music as it existed 100 years ago—a time when people experienced music primarily through attending concerts and listening to informal performances in the parlor. As the trends demonstrate, this is certainly not the case today and is even less likely to be the case tomorrow. It is safe to say that in the future, more people will experience music than ever before, but that 99% of this experience will be filtered through some kind of technology. Should our educational programs continue to be based on only 1% of real-life musical experience when technology offers so many other options?

Prediction #2. The definition of a musician will broaden.

Today, if someone tells us he is a musician, our first reaction is likely to be, "Oh, what do you play?" This is a conditioned response based on two centuries of musical experience in which the term musician became synonymous with performer. However, this idea is a nineteenth century construct and, as the trends indicate, is no longer broad enough to incorporate all the ways people will interact with music in the future. Already, computers, sequencers, and related technologies offer anyone the ability to create pleasing, high quality music without having to perform it. As it becomes less and less expensive to do this, more and more people will begin to explore this creative avenue of musical interaction. The virtuoso *performer* is subsiding in importance, and the *creative* amateur musician is rising.

So too, high quality recording technologies have recently escaped the million dollar studios and come into the hands of ordinary people. It is likely that this trend will not only continue but accelerate. At the professional level over the last 50 years, the studio engineer has emerged as a highly regarded musician in his own right. More and more, ordinary people are acquiring the tools to do the same thing that the professional engineer has been doing, and they are eager for training in how to use them to make more effective music.

Even those musicians who concentrate on performance now have access to tools which allow them to multiply their abilities. As the above trends show, computer interfaces are already available for every type of performer, and these tools explode the traditionally restricted palettes of timbre, speed, range, and dynamics.

Given these trends, should our music education programs continue to focus solely on performance using 200-year-old instrument designs as the culminating experience of music? Or should we instead begin to incorporate creative music making, music reproduction, and more efficient technology-based musical interfaces into our curricula?

Prediction #3. Music making will change, but musicianship will remain constant.

I want to point out that in no part of these two articles about the rapidly changing world of music have I said that *musicianship* will change. Human beings are hardwired for musical response, that is, for the ability to be affected by music. We cannot change this without changing the biological makeup of our species. In the turmoil of accelerating transformation in technology and how we interact with music, the one constant is the musician's ability to communicate musical affect. This means that no matter what medium we use to elicit a response to music—performance, creative music making, music reproduction, etc.—the desire for affective communication is the same. This is what music education should be all about.

Implications

Now, after exploring the trends of current music technology and trying to predict where they will lead us over the next few years, it is time to look at the implications they have on how we should be teaching music now and in the future. No, I'm not going to make specific recommendations. That is for each individual music educator to do given his or her particular environment, philosophical orientation, and understanding of where music is headed. However, here are some overall guides for action based on my own experience:

1. Technology changes the paradigm.

Technology is changing the way we interact with music. It is offering exciting new avenues. broader experiences, fewer restrictions. Those who don't incorporate these technological benefits into their students' musical experiences are depriving them of a modern relevant music education.

2. Imagine the future, not the past.

For over a century, it has been too easy to follow a model of music education based on nineteenth-century musical practice. What is needed today is forward thinking, risk taking, and experimentation with new teaching methods—in short, imaginative approaches to music education based on current realities.

3. Lead; don't follow.

If we wait for someone else to show the way, change will not happen. Each individual must take responsibility for imagining and innovating new approaches matched to his or her own situation. This, incidentally, is one of the most rewarding aspects of teaching.

4. Musicianship remains the constant.

Although it often seems otherwise, the point of music education is not to train people to be virtuoso singers or to build band programs. Rather the point is to bring out in each individual the abilities to understand, appreciate, and express music. Whether these abilities manifest themselves in performance, in creativity, or simply in a deeper response to a musical experience should be irrelevant. We should be, first and foremost, not choir directors, band conductors, or instrumental coaches, but rather music educators.

At the beginning of this new century, music technology is giving us an unprecedented collection of tools for refocusing on this primary goal—if we have the imagination to apply them.

This article first appeared in the Winter 2003 issue of Texas's TMEC Connections. *Reprinted by permission.*

Music Software Programs
Donald R. Tanner

Music software programs are increasing in number. Programs are available for music theory, ear training, composition, pedagogy/performance, sequencing, printing, and many other areas. This article suggests a few of the many available programs that have been used effectively by teachers. These programs represent various types and levels of difficulty.

Composition and Printing
Making Music

Making Music, by Morton Subotnick, is produced by Voyager. It is a program that allows children to compose or create their own music. Making Music presents the components of music visually and aurally, which allows children to be engaged in music through various modes of learning. The program can be used for children of any age and is intended to let them experience composing even before they embark in formal music education. Notation is entered by painting on the screen. The Melody & Rhythm Maker alters pitch and rhythm and enables one to hear how they sound separately and together. Building Blocks transposes or changes simple tunes to learn about the structure of music. Mix and Match combines melody, rhythm, and instrumentation from a varied musical flip book. This program is recommended by some educators as excellent for young children.

The program is considered a CD-ROM Hybrid and works on both Mac and PC. It sells for approximately $39.95 for the consumer version. It is also available in a school version and a 5-lab pack.

Music Appreciation and Music History
Music History Review: Composers

Music History Review: Composers by Electronic Courseware Systems allows users the opportunity to test their knowledge of composers from the Renaissance to the Twentieth Century. Quizzes may be selected from 10 categories with questions presented in a multiple-choice format. Feedback is provided at the end of each quiz. The program allows full record keeping. This disk is coordinated with *A History of Western Music,* 4th ed. (1988) by Donald Jay Grout and Claude V. Palisca, W. W. Norton. Some music educators appreciate the connection with *A History of Western Music"*

This program is available in a single station, a 5-lab pack, a network license, and a site license, and is available for Windows and Macintosh. The single station price is approximately $39.95.

General Music
Music Conservatory

Music Conservatory from Voyetra takes the listener on a musical journey through time as you listen to symphonic masterpieces and learn of the lives and works of great composers, both European and American. This program covers time periods from the Baroque through the Twentieth Century. It helps users gain an understanding of music theory through an introduction to notation, rhythm, tonality, and harmony. Audio and video demonstrations of more than 75 orchestral instruments are available in addition to a music glossary of more than 250 definitions and terms.

This program is appropriate for beginner to intermediate users. Cost of the program is approximately $39.95, and it is designed for PC.

Music Theory and Ear Training
Auralia

Auralia 2.1 from Rising Software is considered to be an ultimate ear training package including melody and pitch, rhythm, intervals and scales, chords and progressions, and many more areas. Auralia 2.1 for Windows covers 26 topics divided into 4 subject areas. Each topic has a system of graded levels and an information screen explaining the exercises. It was designed with a complete record-keeping system as well as an ear-training tutor. Record-keeping results are recorded in a database for later review. Auralia 2.1 is networkable and allows creation of tests. It now includes Sound2 MIDI technology allowing the user to sing intervals or scales into the computer. Auralia will check your answer and tell you if you are correct or incorrect. It

is intermediate to advanced in difficulty and is a challenging program that covers fundamentals.

Auralia for Macintosh is now available. It includes 19 topics and offers a comprehensive ear-training package. Both PC and Mac versions have free sample versions that can be downloaded from the company Web site (www.risingsoftware.com).

This software is available in a consumer version as well as a 5-lab pack and site license for both platforms. For more information, log on to Rising Software's Web site or check your local stores. List price: $149.00.

Musition 2

Musition 2 by Rising Software is a new interactive approach to a music theory and fundamentals package for users of all ages and abilities. It offers drills with instant feedback, creating a stimulating learning environment. Musition 2 also has 25 topics divided into 4 subject areas: note reading, terms and symbols, key centers, and instruments. Its networking and record keeping have been designed to meet the administrative requirements of students, studio teachers, and school-based educators. If you are using Auralia 2, both programs can access the same databases. Musition 2 allows the creation of customized tests. These tests can be shared among all students but with individual test results being recorded. Musition 2 is for PC, list price: 599.00. Also a 5-lab pack and site license are available.

Essentials of Music Theory

Essentials of Music Theory has been released by Alfred Publishing Company, Inc. Designed for ages 8 to adult, it features exercises that reinforce new concepts, narration, and musical examples. It includes a Glossary of Terms with spoken pronunciations plus audio and visual examples of each term. It features scorekeeping of individual scores and students' overall scores. It allows the creation of custom tests. Alfred now offers 3 complete volumes of music theory for a complete curriculum of study. Volume 1 is designed for beginners and covers the staff and notes through note values, flats, and sharps. Volume 2 is scales, intervals, sixteenth notes, triads, and chords. Volume 3 is chord progressions, minor scales, modes, harmonizing, and form.

One can purchase either a single copy or a complete set including Volume 1–3. List price for a single copy is $99.00, and the price for a complete set (Volume 1–3) is $199.95. It is available in 5-lab packs, 10-lab packs, or 30-lab packs. The program is available for both platforms and is an attractive presentation and nicely packaged.

Music Ace 2

Music Ace 2 is the second title in the acclaimed and award winning Music Ace series from Harmonic Vision. This program introduces concepts such as standard notation, rhythm, melody, time signatures, harmony, intervals, and much more. Designed after Music Ace, it uses Maestro Max and his choir to provide many musical examples and a variety of new instruments that advance learning skills in music fundamentals and theory. The program also includes the Music Doodle Pad that gives users creative control over their musical thoughts and a way to experiment with their ideas. This program is excellent and covers a broad scope of material.

Music Ace 2 is available for both PC and Macintosh through a Mac/Win CD. The list price is $49.95.

Music Lab

Music Lab by Musicware is an intermediate to advanced program that helps users learn to sing, read, and write music. The program is organized in a skill development system that can be individually paced. Through a microphone on your computer it interacts with the user in developing pitch matching and sight reading skills. It includes eight interrelated units: sing, notes, names, echo, play, notate, read, and write. Two versions are available: Music Lab Melody and Music Lab Harmony. The student version has no record keeping and is designed for the home. The site-license version includes unlimited record keeping. This is truly a sight-singing program.

It is available for PC and Mac. Music Lab Harmony and Music Lab Melody are approximately $49.95 each.

MiDisaurus

MiDisaurus by Musicware is an award winning music education software series for children from ages 4 to 11. It includes colorful animation, interesting games, and tunes you can play and sing. MiDisaurus, the musical dinosaur, introduces children to the wonderful world of music. It is designed as a user-friendly program and is extremely appealing to children. It uses pictures in association with musical examples to help children relate graphics to sound. Instructions are read aloud as well as given on the screen, thus making it easy for nonreaders. MiDisaurus includes approximately 510 activities that develop skills necessary to read, play, compose, and appreciate music. Teachers have commented that many of the National Standards are addressed.

Available for both platforms, it is efficient for both private teachers and schools. Each MiDisaurus CD-ROM tracks and gives accountability for up to 250 students. Names can be added or deleted before the report is printed. The eight volumes are bundled in two packs: Volumes 1–4 and 5–8. MiDisaurus is reported as an excellent music education program introducing a child to the world of music. The price is approximately $29.95 each.

Sequencing
Home Studio

Home Studio by Cakewalk is a fast, easy way to create music and sound on a PC. It provides online tutorials for a quick start. The program includes a Virtual Piano to play and record music with your PC mouse or keyboard. Editing allows the user to cut, copy, paste, and mix tracks. After editing, music can be printed as sheet music, or saved as an MP3 file for the Internet. Enhanced mixdown options are available providing additional control for preparing CDs or other media. The new Version 9 has a list price of $129.00.

In conclusion, the software packages discussed above can be purchased through your local music store, individual company Web sites, and online music vendors. Here are URLs and phone numbers for software companies mentioned as well as several vendors:

Alfred Publishing Company, Inc.
http://www.alfred.com
1-818-891-5999

Brook Mays Music Company
http://www.brookmays.com
1-800-421-6090, ext. 80445

Cakewalk by Twelve Tone Systems, Inc.
http://www.cakewalk.com/Products
1-888-225-3925

Electronic Courseware Systems
http://www.ecsmedia.com
1-800-832-4965

Harmonic Vision, Inc.
http://www.harmonicvision.com
1-877-576-8742

Lentine's Music
http://www.lentine.com
1-800-822-6752

McCormick's Software Avenue
http://www.mccormicksnet.com
1-800-323-5201

MusicWare
http://www.musicware.com (Web site not yet
serviceable)

Rising Software
http://www.risingsoftware.com
1-888-667-7839

SoundTree Resource Guide
http://www.soundtree.com
1-800-963-TREE

Voyetra Turtle Beach, Inc
http://www.voyetra-turtle-beach.com
1-800-233-9377

Some of these software programs offer a demonstration version that can be downloaded. Demonstration programs will enable you to make a decision regarding the type of presentation and the level of difficulty. Enjoy these varied and helpful programs and the positive advancing technology they represent.

This article first appeared in the Spring 2001 issue of Texas's TMEC Connections. *Reprinted by permission.*

Technology Review
Patricia White

Making More Music by Morton Subotnick, published by Voyager and distributed by Forest Technologies, is an advanced level of the program Making Music. While Making Music is designated for ages 5–10, Making More Music is designated for grades 3–12. The program provides opportunities for students to do creative composition activities with the computer and mouse (no MIDI keyboard needed).

There are 2 main methods of composing: Rhythm Band for nonpitch creations of up to 5 parts and Chamber Music for pitched pieces with 4 parts. For each, the beat is subdivided into 4 boxes, and a mouse click in any box will place a note there. In the pitch section, longer note values may be obtained by dragging the cursor over several boxes. For each staff or track, specific timbres and dynamic levels can be designated.

The program allows entry of up to 200 measures per staff, and allows quarter, eighth, or sixteenth notes as the unit of beat, with 2 to 7 beats per measure. There are several tempo choices ranging from MM = 42 to 240. Key signatures are not used, but melodies are entered as specific pitches on the staff, and scale types, including major and minor, can be selected. Students can enter or view their music in graph or traditional notation (rhythm on a one-line staff) and a moving line follows notation during playback, which can be of a single part or all parts combined. The augmentation and inversion, as well as copy/paste features found in Making Music are also available.

Four other features of this program are Composition Book, where students may save their pieces; Information, which has explanations of basic musical concepts such as pitch and time, as well as a glossary of over 50 terms; the Game section, which has several pitch, rhythm, and form ear-training games comparing audio and/or visual segments; and the Theme and Variations feature, which allows students to take different blocks representing sections of 4 pieces, including Mozart's variations on "Twinkle Little Star," and manipulate them to create their own arrangement.

System requirements: Mac: System 7.1 or higher, 68040 processor, 16 MB RAM, 13″ monitor with 256 color, 2x CD-ROM drive. WIN: Windows 3.1 or 95 with 486 or better; 8 MB RAM, VGA display, 13″ monitor with 256 color, 8-bit Windows compatible sound card, speakers, 2x CD-ROM drive. Hybrid—both versions come on same disk. List: $49.95.

Music Ace 2, published by Harmonic Vision, is a complement to the original Music Ace. Age recommendation by publisher: beginner/age 8 to adult. This is a theory-based instruction and practice program, covering 24 lessons on topics ranging from Lesson One: Beat and Tempo, to the final lesson, Introduction to Harmony. For each lesson, the Professor gives explanation and demonstration of a concept, provides student tasks in order to reinforce the concept, and then provides several games that allow students to measure their skill and knowledge. Explanations give appropriate detail and move in logical sequence, building on earlier lessons. There is considerable audio/visual reinforcement of concepts. Musical examples for each concept are excerpts from standard literature—identified on screen by title and composer. Individual scoring records can be maintained for a select number of students (the specific number needed determines the price of the package).

While the original Music Ace lessons deal primarily with the treble, bass, and grand staff; the piano keyboard; note names; and basic pitch concepts, Music Ace 2 deals with beat, tempo, rhythm, key signatures, time signatures (including compound meter), syncopation, and scales, both major and minor.

Doodle Pad allows students to enter specific note durations—determined by size of the note head versus the more traditional note values—on a staff in order to create their own pieces. This section also has a Juke Box with many prerecorded tunes from folk and classical literature. As any of these pieces play, with different colored notes to represent different timbres, the note head "faces" move to show which notes are being played. This allows children to follow the various parts of a fugue or to see the texture of a more homophonic piece.

System requirements: Mac: System 7.5 or higher; 68040 processor, 12 MB RAM; 256 color, 24 MB free hard disk space; CD-ROM and mouse. WIN: Windows 3.1, 95, 98; 486 66 MHz, 16 MB RAM; 256 color, Super VGA; 24 MB free hard drive space; MPC compatible sound card or Gen MIDI; CD-ROM and mouse. Hybrid—both versions on same disk. List: $49.95 with scorekeeping for six users.

This article first appeared in the January/February 2000 issue of New York's The School Music News. *Reprinted by permission.*

Choosing Software for the Classroom Music Teacher
Donna Williams

Everybody talks about how well music and computers go together. This is certainly true in the professional arena, but in education, the connection is less obvious. Professional music software is expensive and elaborate to use, and usually is out of the range of most school music programs.

I recently took a course on educational technology at The College of New Jersey and was pleased to find alternatives to expensive software written for professional musicians. I was delighted to discover the extent to which music and sound are integrated into many lowcost, children's software programs. With a little creativity, these programs can be used in music classes to engage children in the joy and discipline of musical invention.

Since there are so many programs on the market from which to choose, I thought it would be helpful to provide some pointers on how to select programs which match the music curriculum and how to organize a music class around computer-based activities. In the box, you will find 10 programs which I have successfully used in music classes. Some I listed because they are neat or beautiful and full of color, sound, and music. Some will appeal to limited age spans, while others have enough intricacies for any age. They all provide highly engaging opportunities for children to experiment with music and sounds, listen critically, solve musical puzzles, explore art history, and/or experience musical composition.

What Should I Look For?
I chose the software titles in the accompanying box because they meet the following criteria:

Easy-to-use. I prefer programs which do not require hours of time (my time or my students' time) to learn to use. Can my students access help easily or get suggestions if they don't know where to begin? Is there a "help" icon or a "hint" button which explains how to perform a certain task? Can I give a group direction that everyone will he able to follow? Can a student with a physical disability use this program?

Low frustration producer. Do students get adequate time and multiple chances to work through a problem? Are gentle reminders provided? If the program is a game, do characters get killed or eliminated? Is there a way to start over without restarting the game?

Ease of changing preferences. Can preferences (difficulty levels, speed) be chosen without exiting the program? Do I need to memorize function keys and keystroke patterns, or can I just click on something?

Reading issues. For my students who are nonreaders or non-English readers, a program with little or no reading will facilitate their successful completion of activities. Poor, slow, or early readers, on the other hand, may benefit from a program that requires some reading. I look for programs that highlight words as a voice reads them, such as directions or background informa-

Donna Williams Two Cents' Worth Recommended Software*

Title	Publisher	Music Skills	Comments
ArtRageous!	Softkey/The Learning Company	Art history exploration, elements of composition, art & music connections in history	Share this with the art teacher
Dazzleloids	Voyager	Story with original theme songs by contemporary computer artist R. A. Greenblat	Share this with the art teacher
Julliard Music Adventure	Theatrix	Experimentation, composition, critical listening, theory, puzzles	Students will need instruction time at first; has different levels of difficulty
Lamb Chop Loves Music	Philips	Instruments, sequencing	For young children
Morton Subotnick's Making Music	Forest Technologies/ Voyager	Experimentations, composition, critical listening, theory, puzzles	No reading required; QuickTime 3.0 or later needed for instrument sounds
The Lost Mind of Dr. Brain	Knowledge Adventure/ Sierra	Puzzles, some music history, notation, multiple intelligence theory	Has different levels of difficult; for grades 5+
Thinkin Things 1, 2, and 3	Edmark	Ear training, experimentation (1 & 2), drill design (3)	Classic! (And they're not really music programs)

*Some of these titles may no longer be available for purchase

tion, and allow the student to repeat the reading as needed.

Potential for cross-curricular teaching. Does this music software incorporate information from other subject areas? Can I use this non-music program to teach a music lesson? Sometimes you don't want a program that is strictly music since art, gaming, history, critical thinking, and puzzle programs often incorporate music activities or obstacles, and at the least have theme songs, background music, and rich sound effects (Have you played Myst lately?!) On the other hand, we also need to advertise the way music in general and specifically music software can help students reach developmental milestones, master basic skills, use higher-level thinking, see events in historical contexts, generalize mathematical concepts, etc. No administrator in his/her right mind would call math and reading a "frill;" use their language to inform them why they need this software.

Quality graphics and animation. Any good chef will tell you, "If the food looks good, the person will expect it to taste good." While we all know that it doesn't necessarily mean it is good

for us appearance makes us want to taste it. Students using software are no different. Choose programs with smooth animation, depth of artwork and design, bright colors (especially at the elementary level), and clear text.

Staying power. Choose programs that you can use year after year to minimize your need to replace and upgrade ($$$). Spend your money on a few basic programs with multiple skills levels that will take time for students to complete, then purchase one or two titles a year. Also, rotate programs week to week if possible so they don't get "old" so fast.

Tech support. Do they have a toll free number? What are the hours? The more accessible the company makes itself to you, the more they want and deserve your present and future business. However, it is up to you to know the system requirements of the software and if your hardware can support it before you curse out the technicians.

But I Don't Have a Computer!
Teachers see my enthusiasm for computers in music class and they gripe, "How can I use music software if I don't have access to a computer? I

don't even have a classroom!" But over the years I have learned to problem solve.

My school has a **computer lab**. I jump in it whenever it's free, with the full support of the computer teachers. (By the way, more than once I have heard them doing music activities with students during computer class, which I thought was great.)

Know your school's classrooms. Sometimes bilingual and special education classrooms have computers. Familiarize yourself with what they have and hold a few music classes in their rooms to use the software. If you feel comfortable with the teachers, let them borrow or install a program. Recommend titles that your students have used successfully and enjoyed.

Lastly, I test out new titles in our after school program. Have a music club and include computer activities. When there's a will, there's a way.

Tips for Teachers

I have learned (the hard way) that a clear structure and a few simple rules are necessary to maximize computer-based music activities.

Give students an objective to focus the activity. Start off simply, like "create your own 4-note pattern," then expand.

List what is forbidden. "Do not click on these words: Exit, Shutdown, Save, Delete." Put the list where it is visible. Give a list of alternatives, and help students problem solve when they get stuck. Don't be afraid to exclude someone who does not follow this rule; usually their partners are frustrated also.

Always debrief. Give students a chance to talk about what they have done. Students' misinterpretations of directions can be useful. Ask students who make errors to explain what they did differently from your directions. One of my groups strung together their patterns and created a group song. Unexpected creations can lead to great places.

Cultivate helpers. Second-graders can install and put away CD-ROMs. Older students can supervise younger ones. There's plenty of set up and break down work to do, and students can learn additional skills from helping.

Rules for Students

Buddies are required. Duets, trios, and maybe quartets are acceptable, but no solos.

Sit down or sit out! Students using computers must stay seated at all times, period.

No physical contact. One hand on the mouse at a time. Sit so your legs don't touch.

Summary

Know what you have, what you need, what you can get, and what you will do with it. When you can answer these questions, you will be able to make wise software choices for your school that won't gather dust or make children cry or run away. The best learning takes place when students are engaged and having fun. Good music software choices and exciting computer-based activities can only enhance a strong music program.

This article is reprinted from the May 1999 issue of New Jersey's Tempo. *It originally appeared in the Fall 1998 issue of* TECH-NJ, *from the College of New Jersey School of Education.*

All Tuners Are *Not* Created Equally

Charles Rochester Young

Fundamentals, such as intonation, are critical to successful music making. However, intonation has long been a subject of great confusion and debate amongst musicians. Recently, electronic tuners have been able to provide some assistance, but acoustical knowledge and pedagogical experience do not come inside every package. We, as teachers, must know what the most effective tuners are and how they can be used most effectively towards this end.

Aural and Visual Approaches

The greatest technology ever conceived for improving intonation is the human ear! Great intonation is ultimately the result of critical listening and your ability to match what you hear. The tuner can be an invaluable resource in the development of intonation skills when it is used to sound notes (as another musician would) for you to aurally match. Too often, teachers only use the display window of a tuner to visually show how sharp or flat a student might be. From my experience, the best approach has been to focus primarily on the aural aspects of intonation, using the visual approach secondarily to address any aural difficulty of the student. Ultimately, we need an aural answer, not a visual one.

Practical and Acoustical Justifications

Acoustic tempraments also justify the aural approach. There are two tempraments that we must be concerned with as musicians: just intonation and equal temperament. Though each system has its own unique advantages and disadvantages, both are used daily, whether it be by intuition or design. This means that your students should be able to successfully use both tempraments. Equal temperament represents the modern keyboard, while just intonation represents our human hearing system. Just intonation requires that notes be adjusted according to their relationship to the tonic (e.g., a G-natural would be played differently in the key of F major than it would in the key of C major with regards to intonation), while equal temperament requires no adjustment from key to key (e.g., a G-natural would be played the same in all keys). My students refer to just intonation as being "adjustable" and equal temperament as being "non-adjustable."

The aural approach works for both tempraments, but the visual approach does not! Display windows for most brands are set to equal temperament only, meaning that the visual approach will actually make the student more out-of-tune when playing just intonation! (e.g., a student playing the third scale degree in a major key will play quite sharp if they practice while reading a tuner's equal temperament display window.) Hence, I recommend you buy a tuner whose window can display just intonation and equal temperament values. Furthermore, you want a tuner that can produce pitches for your students to match.

Tuner Features

You want to purchase a tuner that can produce all 12 chromatic pitches in various octaves, allowing you to set any pitch as the tonic. Adjustable calibration is also a must for this chromatic tuner since you may have to play with an out-of-tune piano from time to time! Finally, your tuner should also have audio output and input jacks. This feature allows your tuner to produce pitches into your headphones and/or another sound system so that you can practice at a wide dynamic range without covering up the tonic droning behind you.

Recommendation

To this author's knowledge, the Korg, Peterson, and Coda companies have products on the market with all of these features. Many product manuals from these companies have information on the necessary pitch adjustments for equal temperament and just intonation and many tempraments as well to serve as a resource. At the University of Wisconsin–Stevens Point, we use tuners as part of a larger unit of our own design called a Portable Practice Unit. This unit contains a tuner, a drum machine (for rhythmic development), a microphone, a microphone stand, headphones and a multitrack cassette recorder/mixer. Using this unit a student can record the tuner droning the tonic on track one of the multitrack cassette recorder/mixer, while recording other parts of a piece around it on the other tracks. Since all of their work is recorded, students can monitor and evaluate their progress on an ongoing basis as they add each track..

After several years of implementation, we have found the results to be remarkable. By using responsible pedagogy and high quality equipment, you too will be able to create the teaching and learning environment for intonation that you have always hoped for. Good luck!

This article originally appeared in the December 2000 issue of the Wisconsin School Musician. *Reprinted by permission.*

Digital Audio and Recording Technology

Digital Audio and Recording Technology

Recording Your High School Band or Choir
Matt Anderson

Recording your high school choir or band can be easy and fun; and you may find much of the equipment already available in your high school.

To record a project, you will need a minimum of 3 basic components: microphones to pick up the sound source, reamplification to drive the low-level microphone signal, and a recording medium to retain the recorded sound. When beginning a recording project, it is helpful to preplan your project by determining a few simple choices:

1. Choose a recording medium.
2. Choose your microphones.
3. Decide on a recording space, microphone placement, and setup.

Part I: Choosing a Recording Medium
When you decide to record your choir or band, you will have to decide on the medium you plan to record onto.

Today's world uses two types of recording medium—analog and digital. Analog is where sound is converted into analogous electrical signals and converted back to sound pressure. Digital is where small samples (or pictures) of a sound are captured and then replayed (like the frames of a movie) to reproduce the sound. Your ear then, like the eye in a movie, perceives a seamless recreation of the sound. Analog recording equipment is more readily available at high schools, but digital equipment has greater editing capabilities. While many consumers favor the digital sound quality over analog, it is worth mentioning that many top professionals prefer the "warmth" of analog sound

over digital. Many digital devices now try to emulate the classic analog qualities.

Digital recording equipment tends to be less frequently available in a high school. However, if you have a music budget for the purchase of recording equipment, mini disk recorders such as the Sony MDM-X4 MKII, (retailing for about $700) or hard-disk recorders which use either an internal hard drive or removable media, such as Jaz drives like the Korg D8 (retailing for about $1000) or the Roland VS-840 (retailing for about $900) or DAT (digital audio tape) machines, such as the Tascam DA20 MKII (retailing for about $1000), may be available for digital recording.

Mini Disc recorders are modeled after analog portable studios and tend to have some sort of preamplifier built into their microphone inputs. But, almost all DAT machines, and many hard-disk recorders, will require preamplification to drive the microphone signal. So, you will want to check to see what, if any, additional equipment is needed.

If your school has an auditorium with sound reinforcement (for musicals, etc.) you may have access to a mixing board. If this is the case, you are in good shape. If not, you may wish to speak with your school's audiovisual person about recording equipment or the people who run sound for public events and board of education meetings. Since most mixing boards include preamplifiers, your setup can be as simple as a mixing board, microphones, and a consumer cassette deck.

If you wish to purchase a less expensive analog recording system, you may be interested in portable studios which use an ordinary cassette tape to record all 4 tracks in one direction. Examples of these are Tascam's Porta 02 (retailing for about $160), which is a 4-track recorder able to record only two simultaneous tracks; the Tascam 414 (retailing for about

$290), which is a 4-track recorder; or the Yamaha MT50 (retailing for about $350) another 4-track recorder. Four track cassette recorders almost always incorporate consumer grade preamplifiers to drive the microphone signals. All one needs to do is adjust the input to set the record level.

Depending on which equipment you choose and how you set up, you may need or want to do a mixdown of the recorded tracks into a final stereo cassette. This merely involves setting levels, equalization, and panning of each microphone, and again, will depend on how in-depth you plan to go in your recording.

Part II: Choosing Microphones

Microphones are available in almost every high school. They are used for public announcements at assemblies, board of education meetings, or as part of an auditorium sound system.

A microphone works on the principle of a diaphragm: reacting to sound pressure changes and converting this into electrical energy. The two most common microphones are dynamic and condenser microphones. The basic difference between a dynamic microphone and a condenser microphone is how electrical energy is created in the movement of its diaphragm. A dynamic microphone's diaphragm reacts to sound pressure in a single direction. As sound pressure moves the diaphragm in one direction electrical energy is created in a small coil, and the diaphragm moves back into place to be acted on again by sound pressure. In a condenser microphone, electrical energy is created by measuring the movement of the diaphragm within a capacitor (or condenser) as it vibrates in both directions, both back and forth.

Dynamic microphones are the most common microphones found in a high school. They are most often the microphones used at assemblies and in public address systems. However, if your board of education meetings are broadcast for local cable TV or use sound reinforcement, you may have access to some quality condenser microphones.

Here are some differences between dynamic and condenser microphones:
a. Condenser microphones have more detailed, transient response. Because of this, they tend to make speech more intelligible and, therefore, better for vocal recording.
b. Condenser microphones require an electrical power supply to power their circuitry known as "phantom power." Phantom power is supplied by batteries or from a mixing board or preamplifier driving the microphone signal. If you

have access to a mixing board at your school, you will most often find a phantom power switch in the back by the power switch. This will then send phantom power from the mixer through the microphone cable to the microphone without additional connections or equipment.
c. Dynamic microphones are better able to handle loud sound pressure levels. This may make them more appropriate for close-miking band instruments. However, they tend to be less responsive in their extreme upper and lower frequency ranges.

Besides these differences, it is a good idea, when choosing a microphone, to look at the frequency response of that microphone and see if it is appropriate for the intended application. If at all possible, look at the frequency response graph rather than a written specification, since a graph will show the slopes and roll-offs of the microphones response. A chart of common musical instruments and their frequency ranges is shown in figure 1.

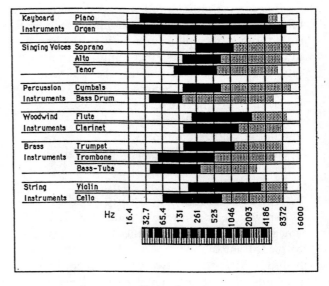

Figure 1

Part III: The Recording Setup

Choosing where to record and knowing a few fundamentals about microphone placement can be helpful in getting the most out of your recording session.

Your auditorium or your classroom will probably be the best choices for a recording space. Your gymnasium, although perhaps being large enough to hold your ensemble, is not usually the best choice. Gymnasiums usually have very poor acoustics, and you can probably remember those

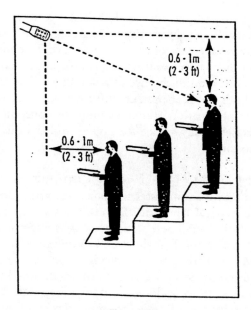

Figure 2

sporting events where the announcer was deafeningly loud, but you could not understand a word that was said. This was because of excessive reverberation from the gymnasium's walls and floor.

Since you will probably be recording multiple sound sources with only a few microphones, it is important to know some simple fundamentals of microphone placement.

Microphones will interfere with each other, causing certain undesirable side effects, such as comb filtering, unless the "3-to-1 rule" of microphone placement is observed. The distance between microphones should be at least 3 times the distance from each microphone to the intended sound source. For example, if you have 2 microphones and you place 1 microphone 5 feet from a group of sopranos in a choir the micro-

phone you place 5 feet in front of the basses should be no less than 15 feet from the microphone on the sopranos.

If you plan on using a single microphone, you can optimally record up to about 20 people standing in a rectangle or wedge shape. Place the microphone a few feet above the heads of the first row (assuming the choir is standing on risers), centered and pointing at the last row (figure 2).

Quite often, particularly with church choirs, it is desirable to capture some of the room ambience by placing one microphone farther away from the sound source. As you move a microphone away from the sound source, direct sound decreases. However, ambient sound always stays the same. If a microphone is moved too far from the sound source, ambient sound becomes dominant, and you may begin to introduce phase cancellations into the recorded sound. This is why you will need to determine the "critical distance" between the direct and ambient sound. You will have to listen through headphones to monitor your microphone's sound to determine optimum placement.

A couple of pictures of microphone placement for a choir can be seen in figure 3. The concepts are the same for instrumental groups.

Recording can be fun and educational for yourself and your students. If you enlist the help of fellow teachers, such as your building's audiovisual person, you might not only find the equipment available in your school, but you may find someone to help you with all the "gozintas" and "gozoutas" of choosing and connecting audio equipment.

This article originally appeared in the May 1999 issue of New Jersey's Tempo. *Reprinted by permission.*

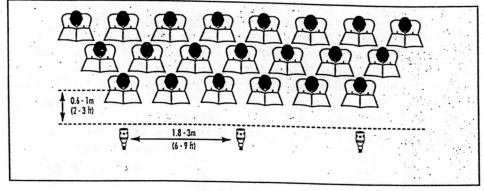

Figure 3

'My Dog Ate My Disk'
D. Larry Bachtell

One of the most frustrating experiences for high school theory and composition students is the inability to hear their works performed as written. Few high school students have the luxury of having ensembles ready and willing to perform their assignments. Thanks to Prince Esterhazy, Haydn had a complete orchestra at his constant disposal; high school students are rarely so lucky. A computer, sound card, or MIDI keyboard, and notation software, however, give every student access to a performing ensemble.

But How's It Going to Sound?
To teach instrument arranging, I frequently hand my students a short piano composition and ask them to arrange it for several instruments. The minor variation from Mozart's *Variations on "Ah, vous dirai-je, maman"* is an interesting work to use as the basis for a woodwind ensemble. Before the advent of computers, the students were able to complete this assignment with little difficulty. The project takes on more vitality, however, when the finished product can be played using the correct timbres. Not only is this far more motivating, but it also helps students identify the best range for each instrument. The immediate aural feedback offered by a computer is especially helpful in more ambitious assignments.

Of course, it would be better if these works could be played by acoustic instruments. Is it realistic, though, to try to gather the necessary players to perform each composition written by every student? Is a music teacher's schedule so free that he or she can spend days supervising instrumental ensemble rehearsals? Can pianos fly?

One caveat: students must be aware that keyboards and soundcards give unrealistic capabilities to orchestral instrument sounds. The true range of each instrument must be known by each student because a computer sample of an instrument can produce tones that are not possible on the actual acoustic instrument. To instructors, this is obvious; to students, this must be taught. Most computer programs are not smart enough to flag incorrect instrument ranges.

But if It Sounds a B-Flat, Why Not Write a B-Flat?
Although notation software can easily perform instrument transpositions and extract parts for individual instruments, I believe that students should be taught how to do this. A young composer will not always have a computer at his disposal to take care of the "grunt" work. Teaching instrument transpositions is a simple matter and does not require the use of a computer. Traditional methods (teacher presents information, students copy information, students complete transposition exercises) easily suffice for giving students the basic tools.

But I Don't Have Twenty Computers!
Don't have a computer in your classroom? Don't have a MIDI keyboard? Don't have a sound card? Don't despair! These items are not as expensive and out-of-reach as they used to be. An adequate IBM-compatible or Macintosh system can now be acquired for less than $2,000. Multi-timbral keyboards are also no longer only for the wealthy. Wavetable sound cards for computers can now be purchased for less than $300. One system in place can form the basis of a very usable music tutorial workstation in your classroom.

One computer system for 20 students might seem absurd—almost like trying to teach 20 kids to draw with one canvas and one set of paints. Believe me, it can be made to work. In getting students to work with a notation program, the biggest obstacle to overcome is introducing the software itself. Most kids are already computer literate and will have little hesitation in working with this technology. To facilitate the introduction of the software, consider using a computer-to-TV interface. This device sends the computer's output to a computer monitor and a television monitor simultaneously, allowing large group instruction to take place. Such devices can be purchased for less than $150.

But Don (or Tom or Dick or Harry) Says that Finale is Better!
The actual notation program you use will depend on your budget and your personal preference. The most popular programs continue to be Finale (IBM Windows or Mac) by Coda, Encore (IBM Windows or Mac) by Passport Design, and Music Printer Plus (IBM DOS) by Temporal Acuity Products. My students have gravitated to Encore as their program of choice. They like its intuitive interface and find it fairly easy to use. The selection of a notation program is a very personal matter. I've been flamed on the Pepper Network for my failure to recommend Finale, but I've also been known to prefer Korg keyboards and Ensoniq sound cards. If you disagree with my

preferences, that's your privilege. (You probably have definite opinions about which of the three tenors has the best voice.)

To return to the basic question: can 1 or 2 computers really be of value with an entire classroom of students? With careful scheduling and supervision, yes they can. Don't allow students to place their files on your hard drive. Give each student a floppy disk for his or her personal files. Insist that the disk stay in the classroom (They may copy the disk if they want to work at home.) Establish a rotation schedule for computer time in class and publish other available times. (They may work on the system while you're teaching another class.) The major crunch for my students occurs on due days. Although I have two printers for their use, my students prefer using the ink jet printer rather than the "old" dot matrix printer. Printing music is time consuming, but the professional appearance of printed scores makes the wait worthwhile.

How Can I Grade It if I Can't Read It?

One of the nice ancillary benefits of using notation software is the legibility of student submissions. Most notation programs give "engraving" quality output. Think of it—no longer do you have to spend half your time trying to decipher a student's manuscript. Assuming that the student has saved his or her work on a disk, you can feel free to indicate corrections, suggestions and other remarks on the page without ruining the "good copy." Once the student has seen your marks, he or she can reload the file, revise it, and print out as many "good copies" as desired. This is particularly useful in building student portfolios for college interviews or (trumpet fanfare, please) for the brave new world of Outcomes-Based Education. (No more excuses of "My dog ate my project" either.)

There are few composition assignments that cannot benefit from using notation software. Harmonizing melodies and writing four part chorales become easier, particularly if the student lacks proficiency at a keyboard to play his sketches. Composing Alberti bass lines or other accompaniment figures becomes easier when students have the ability to experiment with various styles.

By placing sample phrases on each student's disk, experimenting with melodic phrase structures can easily be accomplished. The student can compose multiple consequent phrases and select the most effective after testing each one. The same can be done with harmonic structures and simple forms. Students can experiment with improvisation using similar techniques.

Can I Play Games, Too?

Naturally, you won't want to restrict computer use to notation. The software market is filled with worthwhile programs designed to review and drill basic music skills and concepts. Ear training programs range from simple interval drill (Play It by Ear) to 4-part progressions with inversions (Harmonic Progressions). Characteristics of the basic style periods are presented in Midisoft's Music Mentor. If you're lucky enough to have a CD-ROM drive in your computer, your kids will enjoy working through the various composer oriented disks. Available programs range from Beethoven's Ninth Symphony to Stravinsky's *Rite of Spring*. For sheer fun, let your students explore Microsoft's Musical Instruments. (Everyone should get to hear what a didjeridu sounds like.)

If you want your students to experiment with formal structures and phrase groupings, check out Midisoft's MusicMagic Songbook. This program includes over 100 compositions stored as standard MIDI files. Students can load in a Bach invention, follow the score as it plays, and then rearrange the elements to experiment with different structures. (This is great fun for teachers, too.)

The ubiquitous (and incredibly inexpensive) Band-in-a-Box has some interesting uses for theory students. Students enjoy writing works using jazz harmonies, but they frequently lack the skill to notate stylistically correct piano parts. Let the kids enter their chords into Band-in-a-Box and generate an accompaniment. Save the file as a standard MIDI file and then load it into your notation program. Now the students can see what a jazz-fusion-funk-whatever piano score would look like. This gives them a model for creating their own keyboard parts.

Using a computer in a music theory classroom does force you to be very flexible. Computers do, on occasion, crash and render themselves totally useless. (This usually occur 24 hours before a major project is due, reducing both you and your students to blathering refugees from the World Twelve-Tone Festival.) Encourage your students both to save and print out copies of their work on a regular basis. A few extra minutes spent on these tasks can save you hours in case of difficulty.

The advent of computers in music classrooms has given us wonderful new tools (and, as my wife constantly reminds me, toys) to help our students. You and your students can find many valuable uses for computers. Always keep in mind that the computer is a means, not an end. Pull the plug if your kids are spending more time on computer problems than they are on musical problems. As in all music, what matters most is the sound of a work, not its appearance.

This article first appeared in the March 1995 issue of Pennsylvania's PMEA News. *Reprinted by permission.*

Digital Audio for Music Educators: Part I
Mark Frankel

LPs, cassette tape recorders, Dolby NR. These are the buzzwords of a bygone era. Words and codes like MP3, WAV, and CD-ROM are their successors. The way the world experiences music has always been in a state of flux, but since the advent of digital technology and the PC, things are changing more rapidly than ever. With the massive proliferation of user-friendly software, inexpensive equipment, and a built-in distribution network known as the Internet, it has never been easier to create, record, distribute, and listen to music. Let's take a closer look at the various components needed to get the most out of your computer without spending a fortune.

Not too long ago, everything was analog. Music was (and sometimes still is) recorded magnetically by tracing sound waves and playing them back in a similar fashion. Then, in the early 80s, the compact disc was introduced and it revolutionized the music industry. Still, some don't understand what it means to record and playback digitally. Here's a simple, albeit vague explanation: in essence, digital recording breaks up the audio stream into small, consecutive fragments or snapshots called samples, assigning each one a binary number (a number consisting of two numerals, 0 and 1). Each digit is referred to as a bit. According to the Compact Disc standard set by the Audio Engineering Society, the samples are taken 44,100 times per second (measured in Hertz) and each sample is 16 bits long. Thus the CD specification of 44.1 KHz/16-bit was set.

How does all this benefit audio fidelity? By assigning code to the audio stream, it allows the music to be copied time and time again with no loss; the code is simply read, rewritten and played back without any degradation at all. Also, it records and plays back without introducing any noise. With vinyl LPs and cassettes, the recording and playback mediums themselves generated a certain amount of noise known as the noise floor (heard as hiss, crackles, and pops). With quiet musical passages, often this noise floor is louder than the actual music. While some argue that the CD audio standard lacks the fidelity and musicality of analog equipment (failing to mention how expensive top quality analog gear is), there is no denying that for most people, recorded music has become much clearer and more enjoyable to use and listen to.

It's no surprise that computers would come into play in this digital music revolution, as they process information in the same way as CD players: digitally, using binary code. Thus, the merging of digital music and the home PC was inevitable, but didn't become common until recently, as the freshman attempts were costly and at times, unreliable. However, music software and hardware have been refined and are less expensive than their predecessors, and sound better, too. So as musicians, we are now faced with the problem of too many options. Here are some of the better ones.

Let's use this model: a band teacher wants to record his or her spring concert in stereo and put it on a CD. First, we need a pair of good microphones. All things being equal, microphones play the most important role in the audio chain. A good microphone makes up for mediocre recording equipment, but a recording with a cheap microphone can never sound good even when used with the finest recording studio gear. Look for microphone brands like Sennheiser, Neumann, Earthworks, Oktava, AKG, and Audio Technica. You'll need a pair of identical microphones; one for the left and one for the right channel of the stereo recording.

Next, you'll need some kind of digital recorder. The most common formats are Digital Audio Tape or DAT and MiniDisc, a stand alone hard disk recorder or your computer's hard drive. You don't necessarily need a stand-alone digital recorder, as your computer (which you need anyway) can be used to record as well as edit. An advantage of stand alone digital recorders, though, is that you can archive your recordings without taking up valuable hard drive space. Either way, brands like Tascam, Macintosh, Sony, and Yamaha are recommended.

Regardless of which option you choose, you'll need some kind of microphone preamplifier, which can either be built into the recorder or found externally in a mixer. I would stick with an external microphone mixer like a Mackie, as you'll have more options to adjust the sound, such as EQ.

Once the music is recorded, you have to transfer it into your computer, if you didn't record directly to it already. You'll need some software and hardware to do this. A great stereo editing software, Peak, is made by a company called BIAS. Also, Pro Tools by Digidesign is widely used and you can get a free version off of the Internet from www.digidesign.com. I recommend audio cards and hardware, also by Digidesign and Digigram, for stereo capture of digital audio using a Macintosh computer, G3 processor or higher. You'll need a big hard drive, as 44.1 KHz/16-bit digital audio takes up 10 MB of space per minute, with a full length CD taking up 740 MB or 3/4 of a GB.

The music must then be saved in one of these file formats: .aiff, sd2, or with a PC, a .wav file. These are the formats that CD-R burning software recognizes as a CD audio file. As far as CD burning software, try Toast or Jam by Adaptec, and for CD-R burners, manufacturers like Yamaha and Philips are good names to stick with. Be sure to use quality CD-Rs such as Quantegy or Mitsui.

While we're on the subject of CD-Rs, it's important to point out what they are, technically. The name is an abbreviation that stands for Compact Disc-Recordable. It is not identical to a standard store-bought CD. With the store-bought version, the binary code that I mentioned earlier is represented by the presence or absence of tiny recessed pits. The laser that reads the disc interprets the reflected light to determine if a pit is or isn't present. With a CD-R, a heated laser burns a shaded spot in a dye mat on the CD-R to trick a CD player's laser into thinking it sees a pit. Essentially, to a CD player, a CD and a CD-R are indistinguishable from one another. Though older CD players whose lasers may be slightly out of focus may have trouble reading a CD-R.

Along with standard digital recording formats, data compressed formats such as MiniDisc and MP3 are very common. Both use a method of not recording bits considered to be the "least significant"; in essence disregarding information that you probably wouldn't hear anyway. The benefit of

this is that you are able to fit more information in a smaller space. You'll notice that MiniDiscs are much smaller than CDs and MP3 files take up a fraction of the hard drive space of a standard CD audio file. Another benefit is faster data transmission. Because MP3 files are smaller, it takes less time to transfer them to other computers via the Internet. The trade-off is decreased audio quality. If you are mainly listening to music with a narrow dynamic range such as rock or pop, you may never notice this drop in fidelity. But, if you listen to more classical and jazz, you may notice that the fidelity on the quieter passages is diminished; one may describe the sound as "grainy."

For encoding and decoding MP3s from other audio formats for the Mac, I recommend iTunes, a free Apple product. Other applications such as SoundJam do a good job, too. For your IBM PC, WinAmp is recommended. Once you've encoded your MP3, it's easy to e-mail it to other users or post it on a Web site. It's really very simple and the most common way that music is exchanged on the Internet.

So, you want to do it? Cool. Here's a recommended setup with pricing. For the sake of brevity, I've listed only the major components; stands, cables, and some other accessories are not listed. This setup does not include the stand-alone digital recorder, as I decided to go with a direct-to-hard disk system for this example. All pricing is suggested retail:

- 2 Neumann KM 184 cardioid condenser microphones, $749 each, $1458 total
- 1 Mackie 1202 mixer, $459
- 1 Digidesign AudioMedia III computer interface card, which comes with Pro Tools recording/editing software, $545
- 1 Power Mac G4/466 MHz processor with 384 MB of RAM and a 30 GB hard drive, $1394 (without monitor)
- 1 Yamaha 16X CD-RW recorder with Firewire connection, $320
- Adaptec Jam CD writing software, $199
- Total cost of system, $4375.

Considering the quality of this system (and that it includes the cost of a computer), the price is reasonable. And, it's a fraction of what it used to cost to get the same quality in your end result.

This article originally appeared in the October 2001 issue of New Jersey's Tempo *under the title "Understanding Digital Audio." Reprinted by permission.*

Digital Audio for Music Educators: Part II

Mark Frankel

In my last article in the October 2001 issue of *Tempo*, I gave a basic overview of the various equipment needed to record digitally and create a CD-R, providing some elementary theory about the process along the way. This time, I hope to get a little more in-depth into how to make a good-sounding recording once you've acquired all of the necessary components.

Here was what I suggested you should get equipment-wise in the last article with some updated modifications:

- 1 Shure VP88 stereo condenser microphone, $1,194
- Mackie 1202 mixer, $459
- Sennheiser HD 280 sealed monitoring head-phones, $199
- Digigram VX222 PCI stereo sound card, $549
- Peak two-track editing software by Bias, $499
- Apple Power Mac 800 MHz PowerPC G4, with 256K L2 Cache, 128MB SDRAM memory, 40GB Ultra ATA Drive, CD-RW Drive, $1599 (without monitor)
- Adaptec Jam CD writing software, $199.

To assemble these components, we need to understand the signal path, or route that the audio signal follows from the actual acoustic event to CD-R (see figure 1). First, the sound hits the stereo microphone, then via XLR cables connects to 2 microphone inputs of the mixer (the stereo mic has 2 separate outputs, left and right). From the mixer, the signal passes out of the master outputs and connects to the inputs of the sound card, which is installed in the computer. It is at this point where the analog signal is converted to the digital domain, where it will remain until playback. While in the computer, the digital audio is written to the hard drive, and a file is created. This file(s) is then processed, edited, and a CD-R is made in the CD-R burner.

Now that we have a better grip on how all this stuff gets connected, we can take a better look at how to use it. However, like most anything else, there is skill involved, which develops over time with practice and experience. As you get faster with setting up the gear, troubleshooting, and using the computer to record, your ears will also develop. Over time, you will be more aware of what sounds good and what doesn't. Either way, you'll be miles

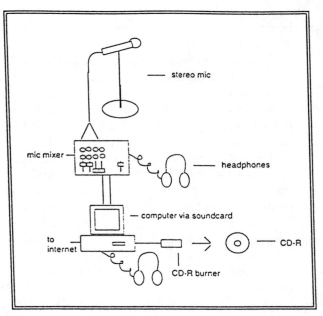

Figure 1

ahead of the sound you got off of your old cassette recorder with a built-in mic or trying to salvage audio from a video camcorder recording.

Placement of the mics (along with proper mic selection) is widely considered to be the most crucial aspect of getting a good recording. While this is a science in itself, here are some tips to get you started:

- **Performance space.** While sometimes this is out of your control, try to record in a room that has plenty of space to let the sound reverberate naturally. Avoid recording in small, boxy rooms with parallel walls and too many reflective (hard) surfaces, such as classrooms. Auditoriums, theaters, churches, larger homes with high ceilings, and even office building lobbies can be great places to record, either with or without an audience.
- **Stereo placement.** I have chosen a one-point stereo mic to capture the audio, as stereo placement with two microphones can be tricky, and may be more of a hindrance than help for a beginner. As you progress, you may want to consider getting 2 separate condenser mics, in which case I recommend a pair of Neumann KM 184s. The Shure VP 88 mic allows you to select different angles of stereo pickup. Try experimenting with the different angles, remembering that a wider pickup angle is better at a closer range, while a narrow angle is better when you're at a distance.
- **Mic location.** Many factors come in to play when deciding where to place the mic in the space that you're recording in. In a more reverberant room, if you are too far from the musi-

cians, the recording will sound too reverberant and lack definition. If you are too close, though, you risk making the recording sound too "tight" or lacking natural reverberation. For example, with a string quartet in a medium-sized room, try placing the mic about 6' high and about 10' away. With a live performance, the audience may force you to place the mics in a less than ideal spot because the mic stand may be obtrusive. As a general rule, try to get the mic up high (10') in the center of the room, about 3 or 4 rows into the audience. A heavy-duty mic stand with extra extensions may be necessary to achieve this.

Once you placed the mic in the space, you need to connect the rest of the equipment to make your recording. Try to get long mic cables, 50' or more, so you can get as far away from the sound source as possible. This way, you be sure that you're hearing your mics, not the actual sound source. Because we're using a stereo microphone, it comes with a special mic cable that connects to a breakout "Y" cable which separates the signals to left and right. Plug the left side into the first input on the Mackie 1202, and the right side into the second input. Set the input gains or trims so that at the loudest part of the music, the meters hover around 0 dB. Both channels should be at the same level. Set the pan control all the way left for channel one and right for channel two. Bring the channel faders to 0 dB, or unity gain. Set the master fader to 0 dB also. Avoid using equalization (EQ), as with a simple stereo recording, mic placement has the most dramatic effect in terms of the sonic quality of the recording. If needed, though, consider reducing the low frequencies a little and boosting the high frequencies even less. Overuse of EQ can make a recording sound unnatural and lack phase coherence.

From the master outputs of the mixer, connect them directly to the inputs of the sound card. Follow the directions for using the sound card, but one thing to make sure of is that the digital sync is set to "internal." Launch Peak, the recording/ editing software, and set up a new file, making sure that you've allotted enough hard drive space to record the audio. As I wrote in the last article, 44.1 KHz/16-bit audio will take up 10 MB for every minute you record.

Before recording, watch the input meters and check that they're not overloading. If they are, try reducing the gain at the microphone input on the mixer or reducing the sound card's input gain. As you record, monitor the signal by connecting the headphones to the mixer.

Once you've finished recording, you need to edit the recording to remove unwanted audio and create CD tracks. First, connect the outputs of the soundcard to the 1202 mixer's line-level inputs, keeping the left and right channels separate to maintain stereo. Start editing by dropping "markers" where you think edits might be. Apply fades between the different cuts to make the transitions smooth. You may want to "normalize" the audio file, so that you're ensured that the file's peak, or maximum level, will be at the highest level possible in the digital domain, 0 dB full scale. Otherwise, you're recording may be too quiet, making it necessary to turn up the volume on whatever playback system you (and your listening audience) is using, thus adding noise. You may want to consider adding effects like reverb, noise reduction, pitch correction, time compression/ expansion, but a little goes a long way. Caution should be exercised to avoid making recordings sound over-produced, and thus amateurish. A little compression, though, to get the recording a little louder overall might be a good idea. Regardless, nothing you do to the audio file is permanent until you save it. You have unlimited levels of "undo," so I encourage you to experiment and discover what works and what doesn't. Making the CD tracks is done in a few different ways. You can either capture individual sections of a single audio file, called regions, and make each of those a track; compile several different entire audio files and make each of those a track; or compile a combination of regions and files. Either way, use the program Jam to create the compilation. Adding tracks is as simple as clicking and dragging from one window to another. The program is very intuitive and runs much like a CD player. Here's where you can quickly check for continuity in terms of volumes and time transitions between tracks.

When you're satisfied with the way the disc sounds, just click write disc, and put in a CD-R to burn. That's about it.

If you want to make an MP3 to send out over the Internet, simply open Apple's iTunes, and convert any of the files you've saved into the MP3 format. To make sending these MP3 files quicker and more reliable, I suggest investing in a high-speed Internet connection like a cable modem or DSL. It's well worth the added expense.

This article first appeared in the March 2002 issue of New Jersey's Tempo. *Reprinted by permission.*

Creating Your Own Music CD
Mike Klinger

Wouldn't it be wonderful to have the technology available to be able to record your band or choir to DAT tape at a concert and then plug the DAT into your computer and burn your own CD? Or wouldn't it be wonderful for your general music class to be able to sequence all of their MIDI tracks, sing in the vocal part, or improvise a solo sax part, and be able to burn a CD of your students' compositions? What a tremendous fund-raiser this could be, not to mention the student portfolios it could create. Well, that day has finally arrived! I recently taught a class to music teachers on how to create your own music CDs. I also presented a seminar called "Creating Your Own Music CDs from Start to Finish" at NCCE (Northwest Council for Computer Education) on March 18 at the Seattle Convention Center, so I felt compelled to share with you my findings on this very important topic. Either Macintosh or Windows computers will work for basic digital audio as long as you follow some of the basic recommendations listed below:

- Macintosh Power PC running system software 8.0 or higher (7.5.3 or greater will work on some digital audio software). PCI slots needed if using a digital audio card. Windows '95/98 with a 16-bit (full duplex) sound card installed (e.g., AWE64)
- 64 MB (or more) RAM (the more the better).
- A large, fast hard drive (6–12 GB at 12 ms or better). Digital audio eats up a whopping 10 MB per stereo minute! Ultra-wide SCSI drive is preferred.
- Some method of backup like a Zip or Jazz Drive or CD-RW (rewriteable). The CD-RW method is preferred. You will need to buy a CD-R anyway to burn your CDs, so just make sure it is rewriteable as well.

Once you have determined that your computer has all of the right components to do digital audio, you must then get the proper hardware in place. This includes the actual CD-RW itself and a possible PCI digital audio card (if needed). On Macintosh, if money is an issue and all that you want to do is record directly from an analog mixer into the computer, then you can get by with using the built-in Apple Sound Manager, using the appropriate software, and you will not need a PCI digital audio card. On Windows, you can get by

using the built-in 16-bit sound card if your computer has one. If, however, you are going to use a DAT recorder to get your music into the computer, then you will need to purchase a PCI digital audio card that has digital inputs on it. While you're at it, you might as well make sure it has analog inputs and outputs as well in case you want to record directly from a mixer. These cards will give you great sound quality in your recording and are the much preferred method if you can afford them. Below is a listing of digital audio cards and CD-RWs that I have found to be very effective for both Macintosh and Windows platforms.

PCI Digital Audio Cards:
- Korg 1212 (www.korgusa.com) $749
- DigitalAudio Labs Card Deluxe (www.digitalaudio.com) $595
- Event Electronics Layla $995, Gina $549, Darla $349 (www.event1.com)
- Audiomedia III (www.digidesign.com) $795

CD-RW (rewriteable) drives:
- Yamaha 4416 $549 (external), $449 (internal)
- Ricoh 6201 $499 (external)
- Panasonic Playwright 4080 $449 (external), $349 (internal)
- Hewlett-Packard HP8100 $359 (internal)

Next comes the digital audio software itself. You will need to determine at this point if you will want to record both audio and MIDI or simply audio only. I like the idea of being able to record both MIDI and audio all in one software because it gives me more options for my students, and it's not that much more money. Plus, most of the software comes with plug-in software modules that allow you to add effects like reverb, echo, digital delay, chorusing, flanging, EQ, and much more. Nonetheless, I will list some of the popular digital audio/MIDI software available to you by platform and educational cost.

Macintosh Digital Audio/MIDI Software:
- Opcode Studio Vision Pro (www.opcode.com) $500
- Opcode Vision DSP (www.opcode.com) $250
- Mark of the Unicorn Digital Performer (www.motu.com) $795
- Steinberg Cubase VST (www.us.steinberg.net) $199.50
- Cakewalk Metro 4 (www.cakewalk.com) $169
- BIAS Deck (www.bias-inc.com) $399. This software records digital audio only. However, you can

import standard MIDI files directly into it, sync it up and record it in as a digital audio track.

Windows Digital Audio/MIDI Software:
- Cakewalk Home Studio 8 (www.cakewalk.com) $99 (4 tracks of audio)
- Cakewalk Professional 8 (www.cakewalk.com) $179 (8 tracks of audio)
- Cakewalk Pro Audio 8 (www.cakewalk.com) $319 (128 tracks of audio)
- Steinberg Cubase VST (www.us.steinberg.net) $199.50
- Steinberg Cubase VST 24 (www.us. steinberg.net) $399.50
- Steinberg Wavelab (www.us.steinberg.net) $249.50. This software records digital audio only, not MIDI. However, it contains all that one would need to record, edit, and burn your own CDs!
- Syntrillium Cool Edit Pro (www.syntrillium.com) $299. This software records digital audio only, not MIDI.
- Dart CD Recorder (www.dartech.com) $49. This software is amazing! It records digital audio, renders MIDI files, audio restoration, CD burning software, and MP3 support.
- PG Music Power Tracks Pro Audio (www.pgmusic.com) $29.95. MIDI sequencer and 2 tracks of digital audio. Very simple, affordable software.

Now that you have determined which digital audio software suits your needs, you will need to pick your CD burning software. Before you do this however, make sure to check your CD-RW because most CD-RWs already come with CD burning software. If this is the case, then you will not need to budget for this. The clear leader here is a company called Adaptec. They have been around a long time, and most CD-RWs come bundled with their software. Also, most CD burning software allows for multisession burning (the ability to record one song and then come back on another day and add more) and/or write-once sessions (the ability to put all of your songs onto a play list in the order that you want them to play and record these all at once). I have found that using the write-once method is the much preferred method, and most of the time you will not end up with any problems in burning your CD.

CD Burning Software:
- Adaptec Toast/Macintosh (www.adaptec.com) $99
- Adaptec Jam/Macintosh (www.adaptec.com) $299
- Adaptec EZ CD Creator/Windows (www.adaptec.com) $99
- Steinberg Clean (www.us.steinberg.net) $64.50

Finally, as long as you have gone this far you might as well design, edit and print your very own CD labels. There is a product that does just this, and it is called CD Labeler Kit by Neato $79.95 (www.neato.com). The kit contains a label applicator, set of assorted labels and inserts, design software for both Mac/Win, disc and jewel case templates, and background art for labels and inserts. Everything you will need for creating and labeling your CDs!

Also, you will need to budget for the actual CDs themselves. Most CD-RW companies recommend TDK CD-Rs. You can buy these in bulk at discount stores like Costco for under $20 a box. Rewriteable disks are more expensive ($12–$18 each), but you won't need large quantities of these. Personally, I use Apogee CDs. They are a bit more money ($30/box of 10), but they are extremely reliable.

Whew! Seems like a lot of things to check on just to record your music into a computer. It might serve us well at this point to put together a checklist of sorts to help organize the items that we would need so that all of our bases are covered and that there are no surprises at the end.

Digital Audio Checklist
Computer type
- Windows or Macintosh?
- Does it meet the requirements listed above or for the type of software I am thinking of buying?

Digital audio card
- Do I need a digital audio card?
- If so, will the card that I pick work on my computer? Are there current supported drivers for it?
- Does it come with the necessary cabling, or will I need to budget for this as well?

CD-RW drive
- Do I want an internal or external drive?
- If external, what type and cost of cabling will I need to hook it up?
- Does the CD-RW support making music CDs (redbook audio)?
- What software comes with the CD-RW?

Digital audio software
- Do I want to be able to do digital audio and midi or just digital audio only?

- Is the software that I have selected supported on my computer and digital audio card?

CD burning software
- Do I really need to buy this or does my CD-RW already come with CD burning software?
- Does it support multisession and write-once sessions?

CD labeling software
- Do I need this or does my CD-RW already come with CD labeling software?

I am extremely excited about the possibilities of recordable CDs. What a great technology this is. I encourage you to start simple and work your way up to more advanced levels. You should be able to do this at a very reasonable cost and should have no problems in getting the support and funding needed from your administration if you can present the possibilities to them.

This article first appeared in the May 1999 issue of Washington's Voice. *Reprinted by permission.*

Section 7

Administration and Technology

 Section 7

Administration and Technology

Let Your Computer Help You When You're Scheduling Solo/Ensemble Contest
Ron Jones

It's September, and you're a week or two into the job of your dreams. For several weeks you have been going through your new library looking for those old warhorses, determining what pieces have missing parts, and formulating a list of newer works to purchase. Your new e-mail account is up and running, evidenced by the junk mail being sent to you by old friends. Suddenly, up it comes, the message from the region president announcing the first music meeting. The meeting place is named, along with the date and time. For a fleeting moment anxiety flickers as you visualize the event. You see yourself finally meeting the region icons, whose reputations you know well. And you are anxious to become acquainted with the rest of music educators through whose excellence the region has gained the reputation of being one of the strongest in the state.

The meeting room in the restaurant is filled with educators greeting each other, inquiring about the summer past and the prospects for another successful year. The president calls the meeting to order and directs everyone to the meeting's agenda.

It's a typical agenda: approve the minutes from the previous meeting, treasurer's report, and contest dates and chairpersons. Contest dates and chairpersons. Your name is listed as a contest chairperson. Oh, this can't be true. You don't have time to chair a contest *and* start a new job.

You think you may be sick. It must be a mistake. They're playing a joke on the new guy in town. That's it. It's a joke!

The president is standing, speaking to the members, and he's introducing you to your new colleagues. He's introducing you as the chairperson of the region's high school solo/ensemble contest. You could cry!

The room erupts in an ovation as the music educators stand applauding, grinning from ear to ear, patting you on the back, laughing loudly as they wish you "good luck."

Well, it could be worse. It could be the early 80s BC (Before Computers). Today, with the right computer applications, organizing solo/ensemble can be easy. For some of us sicker folks it is actually fun. Think of it as if you're following a recipe.

The Contest
The ingredients you will need are:
- A copy of the previous year's contest program
- Computer (PC or Mac)
- E-mail (snail mail may be substituted)
- Excel 4.0 or higher (or any version that has the workbook capability)
- Adobe Acrobat Writer

There are 3 parts to this recipe: gathering the information, assigning time slots, and printing the contest program. The application Excel can handle all 3 parts, or other applications may be substituted.

Gathering the Information
First, browse the copy of the previous year's contest program. This will give you an idea how many adjudicators you need to hire. (Hire them now.) Second, the program will help you determine what information you need to gather. For the sake of this recipe, you will need the following: name of participant, instrument, grade (which will be referred to as division), school, name of director, and most important of all, name of accompanist. Some regions like to include the title and composer of works that will be performed. Again, substitutions are allowed.

Once you've determined what information you need, make an entry form and send it to your colleagues via e-mail. Hopefully, they all have e-mail. If not, have them send you a disk with the needed information. Make sure they know to send this information to you as a *text* file. For those who will respond via e-mail, instruct them to tab, not space, between items. The object here is that as your colleagues send you their information, all you will have to do is copy and paste.

You will need to store the information being sent to you. For this, an Excel workbook file is perfect. First, you will need to create a new workbook. In Excel choose "New" from the "File" menu. In the "New" box select "Workbook." Choose the "OK" button. Excel displays an empty "Workbook Contents" window. You will add documents (worksheets) to the "Workbook Contents" window. To add a new document, choose the "Add" button. In the "Add To Workbook" dialog box choose the "New" button. In the "New" box, select "Worksheet." Choose the "OK" button. Excel creates a new document and adds it to the workbook.

You will need a worksheet for each page of the contest program. You will also need a page to store solo information, a page to store ensemble information, and a page for accompanist scheduling. For the purposes of this article title

Worksheet 1: Solo
Worksheet 2: Ensemble
Worksheet 3: Woodwind
Worksheet 4: Brass
Worksheet 5: Percussion
Worksheet 6: String
Worksheet 7: Vocal
Worksheet 8: Accompanist

This can be done by clicking once on a worksheet in the "Workbook Contents" window, then selecting the "Options" button. Type a new name in the "Document Name" window and click OK.

Once the documents are named, you must format each document (Worksheet) to accept the information you will be receiving. To begin, open the document "Solo" by double clicking. You will notice that the document is nothing more than a spreadsheet with columns denoted by letters, and rows indicated by numbers. Beginning in row 1 name each column as follows:

Column A: (leave blank)
Column B: Participant
Column C: Instrument
Column D: Code
Column E: Division
Column F: School
Column G: Director
Column H: Accompanist

Repeat the above procedure for the "Ensemble" worksheet. Use the same techniques to label the columns in worksheets 3 through 7, except start your labels in row 2 and label column A: "Time." (Worksheets 3 through 7 will become the contest program. Leaving row 1 blank at this time will give you space to print the name of the adjudicator and performance room number once that information has been determined.)

When you open an e-mail from a colleague, you will be able to select the contest information for each student, copy it, then paste it into the appropriate document—solo information in the "Solo" document and ensemble information in the "Ensemble" document. Be certain you paste beginning in the "Participant" column. If your colleagues have followed your instructions and used tab rather than space, the information should line up perfectly.

Assigning Time Slots

Now that all of the information has been gathered, it is time to organize the participants into groupings of like instruments, place them with the appropriate adjudicator, and assign performance times. To group the participants you need to sort your data. With the sort command on the "Data" menu you can reorganize data in a database alphabetically or numerically. Obviously, you will want to sort by instrument. Doing an alphabetical sort of the "Instrument" column would result in instruments being grouped alphabetically, but not grouped with like instruments. For example, alto saxophone would sort to the top of the list, and tenor saxophone would sort to somewhere in the middle. Since these instruments would probably be heard by the same adjudicator, a lot of extra time would be used cutting and pasting to bring these groupings together. This is where the "Code" column comes into use. In the "Code" column assign a numeric value to each instrument based on score order, i.e., 1 for flute, 2 for oboe, 3 for clarinet, etc. Now, from the "Data" menu, select "Sort" and sort by the "Code" column, which will group like instruments. Your database should look similar to example 1.

Your next task, now that everything is sorted by

Example 1

	A	B	C	D	E	F	G	H
1		Flutes	Woodwinds	Brass	Strings	Vocal	Percussion	Piano
2	Time							
3	9:00 AM	Debby Jensen	Kate McDermot			Carol Holst	Geri Zanon	Ben Cantrell
4	9:10 AM	Rebecca Pfaff	Amanda Surgeon			Don Clausen		Hannah Dillon
5	9:20 AM	Chris Solberg	Amanda Surgeon					Catherine Pfaff
6	9:30 AM	Jessica Schreiber	Kate McDermot		Nora Petrich	Anne Krabill		Emily Hall
7	9:40 AM	Amanda Surgeon	Jolene Gailey		Otto Smith	Leslie Lewis		Erica Shreiber
8	9:50 AM		Debby Jensen		Otto Smith	Jeanine Selix		Angela Zimmerman
9	10:00 AM	Amanda Surgeon	Kate McDermot		Rosemary Brauninger	Katie Lenoue		Elli Leinart
10	10:10 AM	Amanda Surgeon	Jolene Gailey			Leslie Lewis		Chris Davis
11	10:20 AM	Kate McDermot	Rosemary Brauninger		Carol Holst	Leslie Lewis		Hillary Nordwell
12	10:30 AM	Laurel Madsen	Judy Gruver		JoDee Ahman	Leslie Lewis		Hillary Nordwell
13	10:40 AM	Kate McDermot	Juanita Weissenfels		JoDee Ahman	Kelsey Chance		Justin Brown
14	10:50 AM	Carol Holst	Debby Jensen		Rosemary Brauninger	Leslie Lewis		Jessica Schreiber
15	11:00 AM	Kate McDermot	Addie Ostrowski		JoDee Ahman	Anne Todnem		Sharon Talbot

instrument and in score order, is to copy the information from the "Solo" and "Ensemble" worksheets into the appropriate "Instrument" and "Adjudicator" worksheets. Select all of the woodwind participant cells and copy. Open the "Woodwind" worksheet and paste. Repeat this process until all of the participants have been placed into the appropriate worksheets. If you have more participants than time in a day, simply add a new worksheet. (And don't forget to hire the judge!)

Next, you need to assign times. Excel has a neat feature called "AutoFill." You can automatically create a series by selecting the fill handle in the lower-right corner of a selection and dragging through a selection of cells. Excel continues any series you started in the selection, such as time increments. To create this series, open the "Woodwind" worksheet. Select a range of two cells (A3 and A4) and enter the first two times. Leave the range selected. To extend the selection into the adjacent cells below, drag the fill handle down. Release the mouse button at the end of the series range you want to create. Once the times are in, copy "column A" and paste this column in the remaining "Instrument" worksheets and the "Accompanist" worksheet.

That's it, you're done … in your dreams! Now comes the hard part: finding all of the conflicts. This is the frustrating part, unless you have a photographic memory.

Everyone who has organized a solo/ensemble contest knows that the accompanists drive the schedule. The biggest problem is trying to visualize who's accompanying whom and at what time. Well, this is where putting everything in the database is going to pay off.

If all of the "Instrument" worksheets use an identical time schedule (which they should), and you copy the "Accompanist" column from each "Instrument" worksheet and paste it into the "Accompanist" worksheet, eventually you will be able to look at a single page and observe any conflicts. Unfortunately, when you make changes, you will have to go back and copy the "Accompanist" column from the worksheet you made changes in, and paste the new information in the "Accompanist" worksheet.

There is a much simpler way of accomplishing this—write a formula. Wow! Don't panic. This is as easy as cutting and pasting.

First, open the "Accompanist" worksheet. You should have already copied the "Time" column, column A, into the worksheet. Title column B with the name of your first "Instrument" worksheet, Woodwinds; column C with the name of the second "Instrument" worksheet, etc.

Click in column B, row 3. Type the equal (=) sign. Go to the "Woodwind" worksheet. Select row 3 and drag, stopping at the last entry. Release the mouse button and hit "Enter." Notice that you have been returned to the "Accompanist" worksheet and a formula has been automatically entered. To extend the formula into the adjacent cells below, drag the fill handle down. Presto! All of the accompanists' names will appear.

Repeat this procedure in the remaining columns. Don't forget the equal sign (=). When you have finished, the "Accompanist" worksheet should look similar to example 2.

Example 2

	A	B	C	D	E	F	G	H
1		Participant	Instrument	Code	Division	School	Director	Accompanist
2		Kim Frazer	Flute	01	A	Port Angeles High School	Doug Gailey	Kate McDermott
3		Jesse Golkberg	Flute	01	A	Port Angeles High School	Doug Gailey	Kate McDermott
4		Erica Shideler	Flute	01	A	Port Angeles High School	Doug Gailey	Rosemary Brauninger
5		Heidi Wolfley	Flute	01	C	Roosevelt Middle School	Dennis Degnan	Kate McDermott
6		Kim Madsen	Flute	01	C	Roosevelt Middle School	Dennis Degnan	Laurel Madsen
7		Amanda Surgeon	Flute	01	A	Sequin High School	Vera Fosket	Debby Surgeon
8		Rebecca Westnam	Flute	01	C	Sequin Middle School	Vera Fosket	Amanda Surgeon
9		Kristin Bishop	Flute	01	C	Sequin Middle School	Vera Fosket	Amanda Surgeon
10								

If an accompanist is scheduled to perform for two or more participants at the same time, it is easy to go the appropriate worksheet and adjust the schedule. Any changes made in an "Instrument" worksheet will automatically be changed in the "Accompanist" worksheet.

Once you have all of the accompanist conflicts resolved, send a draft copy of the program to your colleagues.

Ahhh, the Program

Actually, the program is already done. You've got it. The program is the "Instrument" worksheets. With a couple of alterations and a few adjustments made to the "Page setup," (found in the "File" menu), you're ready to print the program.

First, make the changes to the worksheet. Some information contained in the worksheet that was needed for scheduling purposes isn't needed in the program. Determine what information you want to publish. You will certainly want to include the name of the participants and the time of performance but clearly don't need to publish the "Code." For this example choose to publish "Time, Participant, Instrument, Division," and "School."

You will need to relocate the column "Code" to a new column to the right of the "Accompanist" column (column I). Here's how: Select the "Code" column (column D) by clicking the letter on top of the column. A border will appear around the column. Click on the border

and drag the contents of the column to the new location (column I). Select the columns for "Division" and "School" and drag their contents to cells D and E respectively. Next, select the columns and rows you want to print. From the "Options" menu, choose "Set Print Area." Now you're ready for the final adjustments.

Choose "Page Setup" from the "File" menu. See that "Row & Column Headings" and "Cell Gridlines" are not checked. Click the "Header" button. In the box titled "Center," type the name of your contest and click "OK." Do this for each "Instrument" worksheet, and when you're finished, print.

If you have a copy of Adobe Acrobat Writer, you can print your program as a .pdf file, attach it to e-mail, and send it to your colleagues without losing the formatting. Once you have done this, you can enlist the help of your colleagues in identifying student conflicts, which are otherwise nearly impossible to detect. When your colleagues respond, make the necessary changes and presto, you're done.

If you're a nice guy, you will keep a copy of your solo/ensemble database and pass it on as a template to the next poor soul whose turn it will be to host.

This article first appeared in the October 1999 issue of Washington's Voice. *Reprinted by permission.*

Scan Your Way to Better Attendance Control
Bill Naydan

Some of my best ideas for school have come to me in the most unrelated places. My choir has grown over an eight-year period from 55 students to over 180. Attendance and sectional rehearsals were a logistical nightmare. Then a cashier at the Home Depot showed me a better way, and I want to share with you what I did to solve a problem for those of us dealing with large numbers of students on a daily basis.

Someone in front of me was buying bolts, and the cashier took out a master book of bolts and scanned the items with a hand-held barcode scanner. Then it dawned on me—could I barcode my choir? I then began researching the world of barcode technology. The scanners are simply alternate input devices that plug into a "Y" plug with your ps2-style keyboard. There are pen-type, trigger-activated, and barcode-activated types. I settled on an Intermec S Series barcode scanning system. It draws power from your PC to operate and automatically reads a barcode when one is passed below it. It can be mounted on a shelf for ease of use.

The barcode itself is a True-Type font that I downloaded for free from an Internet Web site. It is called Code39 and is a commonly used font. The barcodes must be written with an asterisk at the beginning and end with all caps in between. Commas indicate a space. So the barcode for NAYDAN, WILLIAM would look like this: *NAYDAN,WILLIAM*. I then printed labels for all students once I set up a file with the asterisk format. You need a good laser printer to make the labels on their ID cards. Experience with wear has shown me that a piece of book tape makes the label last a long time.

I then set up a spreadsheet (I use Excel) to check in students. You can code the scanner to do various functions. For this application, automatic carriage return saves the step of manually moving down the spreadsheet. I place an officer at the computer to make sure the "one student, one card" policy is enforced. If a student has forgotten his or her card, the officer codes them in. Now it is the student's responsibility at every class period as well as every sectional rehearsal to clock themselves in. The office now receives an alphabetized list of any rehearsal or lunch period they require, and I can keep a record of all rehearsal attendance when grading time comes along.

We also used the system to input data for District orchestra re-auditions; setting up the scanner to tab feed (go sideways) streamlined the data entry process with a high degree of accuracy and no actual keystroke errors. I even use the barcodes on the student grading cards. It is the best investment I have ever made. Assuming you have a computer and access to a laser printer, the cost of this system for me was $225 plus the cost of a set of laser labels ($15–$30). It was well worth the investment. Now when my kids enter my room for a rehearsal, they have their cards ready to zap themselves in.

This article first appeared in the March 2001 issue of Pennsylvania's PMEA News. Reprinted by permission.

Keeping Track of Students' Records
Donald R. Tanner

Computer software today allows educators to take advantage of some excellent record keeping systems. In fact, you possibly already have this software in an integrated package on your computer. Two specific types of software are useful: spreadsheets and databases. They allow you to streamline laborious tasks into efficient record keeping systems. In this article, consideration will be given to keeping grade books, student progress reports, and various inventories such as instrument and equipment inventories. If you already use spreadsheets and databases, the specific adaptations will be second nature. Otherwise, most software programs have online tutorials that help you become familiar with the necessary tools.

Using an Excel Gradebook
Numerous gradebook programs are available. Some are organized through using a program wizard. These programs usually have embellishments that may or may not be necessary for your particular needs. Some programs are menu driven and include other interesting features. If you are considering such a program, you may want to examine how easy it is to input students' names, assignments, and specific grades for those assignments before deciding to adopt the software. Certain programs keep the records very well, but may not average the grades according to the percentages

allotted for each assignment. If the program allows you to alter the formulas, you may find this useful.

Using a spreadsheet to keep grades is not a new idea. The spreadsheet example in this article uses Microsoft Excel; however, any spreadsheet will function similarly. The example shown in Figure 1 was given to the author by Dr. Edward Anderson, professor of mechanical engineering and associate director of the Teaching, Learning, and Technology Center at Texas Tech University. This particular gradebook has several distinctive advantages incorporated by Anderson (1999).

This grade spreadsheet is efficient and easy to use. It does not use the Excel wizard but rather a blank spreadsheet. The ultimate goal of this particular model is that it can be saved to HTML and exported to your Web site. Figure 1 shows the layout as it looks in the spreadsheet. It includes student names, student IDs, student code names, homework assignments, examinations, current totals, and the final percent and final letter grade. Every time any one of these categories is updated, the entire spreadsheet changes and reflects the current status of that change. It is an efficient way to keep grades current and available for posting.

Students' names are placed first. This particular model uses Column B in order to create an open visual space on the left-hand side. By double clicking on the column divider in the column heading, the width is adjusted to accommodate the length of the name. This feature applies to adjusting all column widths. If you need to supply a student ID, such as a social security number, the ID can be placed in Column D. As you see in figure 1, Column C is left blank to separate student names from ID numbers. When actually using this spreadsheet, you may want to separate all sections such as homework, exams, etc. by a blank column. It is visually more pleasing.

Code names are necessary if you wish to post your grade sheet. Grades cannot be posted either by student name or social security number. Universities and colleges usually provide a random student number that may be used. It is the best policy to check with your administration regarding the regulations on posting grades. I ask students to choose their own code names and sign a statement that allows their grade to be posted on the Web under that code name. When posting grades to the Web, select only the part of the spreadsheet that starts with the code name, thus excluding the student name and student ID number. When posting to the Web, highlight the portion of the spreadsheet you wish to post, and under File, select Save as HTML. Then open that HTML file in Microsoft FrontPage, or whatever program you are using for your Web site.

In this gradebook the H1, H2, and H3 columns represent homework assignments reported with point values. Current Total (Column I) is the total percentage of those three assignments. E 1, E2, and E3 are exams and are reported in percentages. Current Total (Column M) is the percentage average of exams. The Final Exam is a percentage. The Final Percent is a calculation including homework assignments, exams, and the final exam (if the exam has been taken at the time of calculation).

The Final Grade (Column P) is the final computation. These formulas are written to post a Final Percent and a Final Grade for whatever work has been completed at that time.

Across the bottom of the spreadsheet are the

Figure 1

Microsoft Excel - GradeSheet

P6 = =IF(O6>0.9,"A",IF(O6>0.8,"B",IF(O6>0.7,"C",IF(O6>0.6,"D","F"))))

A	Name	C	ID	Code	H1	H2	H3	Total	E1	E2	E3	Total	Final Exam	Final Percent	Final Grade
					Homework			Current				Current			
	Student 1		ID1	Zed	8	7	8	77%	85	85	85	85%	81	82%	B
	Student 2		ID2	Bert	6	7	7	67%	56	65	80	67%	70	68%	D
	Student 3		ID3	Ellie	7	10	9	87%	94	92	95	94%	95	92%	A
	Total Available				10	10	10	30	100	100	100	300	100		
	Weights							25%				50%	25%		

totals and the weights for each category. The Total Available for columns H1, H2, and H3 represents the number of points possible for each assignment (10 points) with the Current Total equaling 30 points. E1, E2, and E3 are exams that are worth 100% each with the Current Total representing the average of the exams. The Final Exam is valued at 100%.

The Weights category (B12) shows the assignments to be worth 25%, the exams worth 50%, and the final exam worth 25%. Formulas are as follows:

Current Totals for Homework: =IF($I$11=0, 0, SUM(F6:H6)/I 11). The "$" indicates the absolute value of "M" and "11" no matter how many rows are inserted in the spreadsheet. The symbol "$" always indicates absolute value.

Current Total for Exams: =IF($M$11=0, 0, SUM(J6:L6)/$M$11). Total Available (I 1 l) is the sum of your homework assignments. The same is true for the Current Total for Exams. No formulas are needed for the Weights categories, as they are simple percentages.

Final Percent (Column O) is the calculation that determines the overall grade. The formula is: =IF ($M$11=0,I6,IF($N$11=0,($I$12*I6+$M$12*M6) /0.75,$I$12*I6+$M$12*M6+$N$12*N6/$N$11)).

The Final Grade (Column P) is derived by the following formula: =IF(O6>0.90,"A",IF(O6>0. 80,"B",IF(O6>0.70,"C", IF(O6>0.60,"D", "F")))).

Excel Checklist for Individual Student Progress

This checklist for individual student progress is one that I designed to keep track of student progress toward student teaching and graduation (see figure 2). At the top is a heading that indicates what degree plan the individual student is pursuing. Other pertinent information such as social security number, TASP scores and date the TASP was passed, the catalog year under which the student entered, and a place to indicate if any college credit was transferred and from what college. A space for the ExCET score is provided to complete the form when the student has completed the program.

In Column A courses are listed according to category. Column B provides a place to indicate transfer work and under what number the work transferred. Column C is the course grade; Column D gives the credit hours; Column E reports the points associated with each letter grade (A = 4, B = 3, etc.); Column F reports the quality points earned (credit hours x quality points); Column H allows a column to average the GPA. In figure 2 you can see that H24 = 3.32, which is F24 divided by D24. As only the courses completed compute in the formula, an instant update of GPA for that particular category of curriculum is provided each time a course grade, hours, and points are entered. In Column J a space is provid-

Figure 2

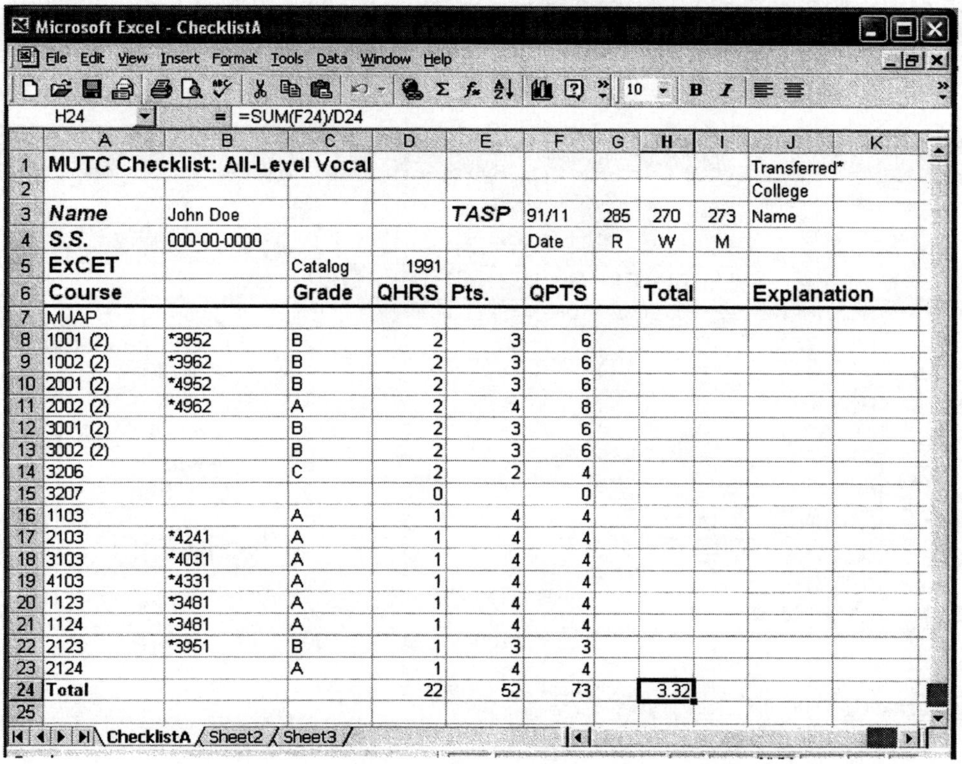

	A	B	C	D	E	F	G	H	I	J	K
1	MUTC Checklist: All-Level Vocal									Transferred*	
2										College	
3	Name	John Doe			TASP	91/11	285	270	273	Name	
4	S.S.	000-00-0000				Date	R	W	M		
5	ExCET		Catalog	1991							
6	Course		Grade	QHRS	Pts.	QPTS		Total		Explanation	
7	MUAP										
8	1001 (2)	*3952	B	2	3	6					
9	1002 (2)	*3962	B	2	3	6					
10	2001 (2)	*4952	B	2	3	6					
11	2002 (2)	*4962	A	2	4	8					
12	3001 (2)		B	2	3	6					
13	3002 (2)		B	2	3	6					
14	3206		C	2	2	4					
15	3207			0		0					
16	1103		A	1	4	4					
17	2103	*4241	A	1	4	4					
18	3103	*4031	A	1	4	4					
19	4103	*4331	A	1	4	4					
20	1123	*3481	A	1	4	4					
21	1124	*3481	A	1	4	4					
22	2123	*3951	B	1	3	3					
23	2124		A	1	4	4					
24	Total			22	52	73		3.32			
25											

ed for any explanation such as when a student is planning on taking a particular course.

Figure 3 reports the end of the second page of the same spreadsheet. Column B is continually used to make a note of courses transferred, substituted, or still lacking. In this section of the spreadsheet, Column J is used to calculate the overall GPA of all courses taken. The music GPA is the calculation of only the courses in the major area. Observation Hours is where the hours of Field Experience are reported, and below that an indication as to whether or not the Teacher Certification plan has been filed.

Figure 3 shows J83 highlighted (overall GPA = 2.88). The formula for calculation is shown in the formula bar below the toolbar column letters. The formula is =SUM(H24+H31+H42+H53+H61+H69+H90)/7. Each of the categories (H24, H31, H42, etc.) provides a summary of particular curricular areas, e.g., music history, music theory, professional development, general education, and others. The degree plan can be divided into categories to keep track of courses easily listed on any part of it. The formula for the music GPA is written exactly the same, except it includes only categories of courses that are in the student's major. This spreadsheet can be adapted for any type of tracking you desire.

Use of Databases

Databases provide extremely useful functions for keeping track of classroom projects. Database programs are available for both computer platforms and both function quite similarly. This article will discuss the general uses of a database in terms of applications that are appropriate. FileMaker Pro (Macintosh) and Microsoft Access (PC) are used as example software programs.

A database helps you locate information quickly. It allows you to update and maintain records efficiently and print documents and reports from your database. A database is like a file folder. Each piece of information about a particular record—for example, name, address, and phone number—is stored in a field. Databases are files made up of related fields. Database programs can store many types of data: text, numbers, dates, times, pictures, sounds, calculations, and summaries. The layout is the way in which data is entered, viewed, and stored. New layouts can easily be created from existing databases.

To make a database effective, it must be designed with a specific purpose in mind. Many layouts display only some of the fields in a database rather than all of them. New designs are created in the layout mode (or whatever it is named by a particular database), and records are viewed in a preview mode. The databases mentioned here automatically save when you leave the record and save frequently while you are working on the record.

It is important to take time to design a database before it is created. Doing this will save considerable time. Even if changes are necessary, it is more efficient to have your model thought

Figure 3

	A				E	F	G	H	I	J	
80	SCIENCE	BIOL 3424	B	4	3	12		Final Calculations:			
81	COMS 2300		B	3	3	9		GPA			
82	EDSE 2300	PSY 4153	B	3	3	9					
83	EDIT 2318	CIS 3023	B	3	3	9		Overall		2.88	
84	HIST 2300	*3373	E	3	3	9		Music		3.41	
85	HIST 2301	*3383	A	3	3	9		Obs. Hrs		78	
86	POLS 1301	LACKING	A		3	0		Cert.		Yes	
87	POLS 2302	*4343	B	3	3	9		Plan			
88	PF&W, Band	*PE 3161	A	1	3	3					
89	or ROTC(2)	LACKING				0					
90	Total			29	34	90		3.1			
91											

through with a definite purpose of intention.

When designing a database, consider the following: what categories of information you will be working with, specifically what you want it to do, what type of information will you want to store in your database, and what layouts will you need. As databases must be designed logically, it is a good practice to lay it out on paper in order to see how it fits together. When you have the basic elements in place, you can begin to identify the needed fields. When designing fields, it is a good practice to use separate fields for first and last names in order to sort more efficiently. Also, use separate fields for city, state, and zip code. When creating fields, identify whether the field is a text field, a number field, a time field, a picture/sound field, or a calculation field. You can add or change a field later by choosing define fields.

By including the same field in more than one database, beneficial relationships can be created. For example, an instrument inventory, can be connected to an individual student's record. In order for this to work successfully, the student record must also include the name of the instrument. By connecting two small databases, it is possible to immediately locate which student has a particular instrument checked out.

These databases connect the student by last name and the particular instrument checked to that student. Many databases have some type of wizard that creates reports or forms connecting various variables. A careful study of the database manual or a tutorial is the best way to develop the understanding you need.

In summary, creative uses of spreadsheets and databases can streamline daily operations in the classroom. By establishing a grade sheet that automatically updates final grades with each new calculation, determining a student's current grade is more accurate and efficient. If teaching in a situation where posting grades to the Web is appropriate, the method allows students to track their progress on a regular basis. Other spreadsheet uses may easily be designated to track varying types of student information.

Databases have traditionally long been used effectively to maintain large and sometimes complex sets of data. Utilization of these databanks can provide thorough and systematic records that will greatly benefit your program and your school.

This article originally appeared in the Spring 1999 issue of Texas's TMEC Connections. *Reprinted by permission.*

Section 8

Why Technology in the Music Classroom?

 Section 8

Why Technology in the Music Classroom?

Can a Computer Do Your Job Better Than You Can?
Jay Dorfman

Introduction

As music educators, most of us feel that our experience, patience, caring, and above all, our musicianship make us the best at what we do. We spend our formative years finding the best and most effective methods of teaching our students, then use the rest of our careers to hone our craft.

In the modern education world, we are constantly faced with new situations that we may either welcome with open arms, or we may choose to turn away from them. Integrating technology into our traditional music classrooms is just such an opportunity.

School districts throughout our nation are currently dedicating large portions of their budgets to technology. Teachers across the curriculum are encouraged to use and teach the technology of their specific field. But while teachers in many subject areas view technology as a time saver, music teachers have been somewhat resistant to the available technology.

Recent research has examined the merits of technology in the music classroom. The focus of much of this research has been to determine to what extent computers or other technological devices can replace traditional methods of music education. The purpose of this article is to examine the results of that research, and to draw some conclusions to help us use technology to our advantage. Is technology an effective tool for today's music teachers? Can a computer do what you do, as well as, or better than you can?

The Research

The use of a game—like piece of software—and its motivational benefits toward music learning were observed and analyzed in a study by Simms (1998). Four male beginning piano students, who all had certain motivational deficiencies toward the acquisition of basic piano skills, were used as the population for this study and were observed using the Miracle Piano System as an alternative means of obtaining minimum performance levels. The author based her observations on Mehr and Braskamp's Theory of Personal Investment, which observes 5 patterns of behavior: (1) direction of attention, (2) level of activity, (3) persistence, (4) continuing motivation, and (5) performance.

As a result of utilizing a technological approach to teaching these beginning piano students, improvements in the 5 observed behaviors were present. Simms concluded that rather than choosing to challenge themselves, students remained at the beginning levels of the program's game-like structure.

The small population for the study allowed the author to make concrete observations about each individual participant, taking into account their initial levels of interest, skill, and motivation (both intrinsic and extrinsic). Four weeks after the conclusion of the study, all students still showed signs of raised levels of interest and motivation and gained the skills that the program focused on during their period of exposure to it. The author concluded that the technological approach used in this study would have long-lasting effects on the students. Of interest would be the comparison of this study to a similar population exposed to the same skills in traditional studio lesson format and a comparison of the lasting motivational effects of each.

Repp (1999) studied technological methods as they related to applied voice lessons of undergraduate students. Three types of technology were employed in this study: (1) accompaniment software (SmartMusic), (2) Internet functions such as the World Wide Web and e-mail, and (3) spectral analysis software. These types of technologies were used in each of 8 45-minute voice lessons for 6 students.

Students were exposed to the technology both in the lesson setting and outside of the lesson. The author collected 3 forms of data, only 2 of which measured the effectiveness of the technology. The students were asked to complete questionnaires regarding their reactions to the technology at the end of each of their 8 lessons. Then, students completed an online Likert-style questionnaire about the effectiveness of the technology implementation outside of the lesson environment. Finally, the author, who was also the voice teacher, recorded a journal of his own reactions to the uses of technology in his studio.

The spectral analysis portion of the data collection proved to be less effective over time. The author concludes that this portion of the study was effected by the "novelty" of the analysis device. Students found it interesting and useful at the beginning of the study, but their interest waned as the semester progressed.

The integration of the Internet into lessons proved slightly more favorable throughout the course of the study. The author reported problems of students not checking their e-mail regularly and the speed of Internet connections in his studio as a hindrance to this technique.

SmartMusic software contains functions for accompaniment, a chromatic tuner, and a warm-up device that allows user-controllable pitch selection through a footswitch attachment. All three areas of the software were employed in this study, and each proved a feasible tool for use in and out of the studio setting. The author says that the software is relatively inexpensive and easy to use, securing the status as appropriate and feasible in both environments. The author intends to repeat the study in a future semester using other types of technological tools.

Bush (2000) studied the effect of hypermedia on learning style and gender. The author first organized the population for the study into groups using the Group Embedded Figures Test (GEFT), a test that measures the degree to which subjects are affected by the organization of data with which they are presented. This test reveals two groups: (1) Field dependent (FD) individuals are influenced by the organization of data with which they are presented; (2) Field independent (FI) individuals perceive elements embedded within a background. Test results placed 41 students in the experimental group and 43 in the control group. Subjects (N = 84) were sixth- and seventh-grade Canadian music students.

During the two-week data collection time, experimental group subjects had 40 minutes to review the hypermedia lessons about steel drum ensembles that the author had compiled using Hypercard 2.2, CD Audio Toolkit, and other scanning and utility software. Students also received a tutorial about how to use the hypermedia lessons. A 40-minute lesson was presented in more traditional lecture format to the control group that included the same information as the hypermedia lesson, and in fact used the same video and audio clips. By the end of the two-week time period, each student had been given a 20-question multiple-choice test about the information in the lessons. The post-test was readministered six weeks later.

The data indicated significant differences in test scores. The control group that did not use the hypermedia lessons scored higher than the experimental group. The students labeled as FI scored higher than those who tested as FD. Test scores dropped significantly between the two administrations. There was no significant difference in test scores between males and females.

The differences between the experimental and control groups may be due to a lack of validity in the testing instrument. Bush refers to previous research that claims no significant differences between the achievement of students who learn using the two different methods and is therefore surprised by the outcome of his study. The "richer learning environment" used in the hypermedia instruction may not be compatible with the author-designed test.

The variance between the scores of FI and FD supports research that when exposed to hypermedia material, field independent students will score higher than control groups. The lack of significant differences between the test scores of male and female subjects for both the first and second post-tests indicate that males and females, "are equally capable of learning in a music classroom through hypermedia and traditional instruction." The author also includes his observation that the hypermedia instruction used less classroom time than did the traditional expository teaching.

Bush suggests that further research is needed in the area of long-term retention levels of students who are exposed to hypermedia, and that a longer testing instrument may have rendered different results.

Orman (1998) studied the use of technology as a replacement for traditional instruction for beginning saxophone students. An experimental group of 20 sixth graders used a computer program designed by the author using Macromedia's Authorware Professional for 8 to 15 minutes a day over a period of 15 to 17 days. The program contained 11 instructional units relating to various topics of interest to beginning saxophonists. A control group of 24 students was not exposed to the program, but instead had only traditional instruction. Upon completion of the computer program, the experimental-group students were given a Lykert-type survey that examined their attitudes toward the program. Both groups were given a post test regarding the information they learned during the time of the experiment. Also, students were videotaped demonstrating their abilities to assemble and disassemble their instrument, and the performance of long tones.

Attitudes toward the computer program revealed that the students were in favor of the program's use. The post-test data indicate that students who used the computer program learned the information better than those in the control group. The videotape data, as analyzed by 2 experts, revealed that the computer-instructed students were more successful than the traditionally-instructed students in the executive skill areas.

From these analyses, the author concludes that similar types of multimedia programs would be effective for use in other areas of instrumental music education.

Meeuwsen, Flohr, and Fink (2000) used a computer program to help predict the rhythmic abilities of 30 students who were from various elementary schools in the Denton, Texas area. The program, designed by the authors, was designed to test the rhythmic abilities of those students to perform in synchronization with prerecorded MIDI excerpts and to retain and imitate similar excerpts. Subjects took the test twice over a two-week period.

The Rhythmic Performance Test-Revised (RPT-R) was theoretically based on the Rhythmic Competency Analysis Test (Weikart, 1989). The first part of RPT-R was designed to test rhythmic synchronization by playing an Irish folk song at varying tempi; the second part was designed to test imitation by playing 20 rhythm patterns of varying length, meter, and tempo, to be imitated by the subject.

The data collected were measurements, in milliseconds, of the subject's deviations of accuracy. Three types of deviation measurements were collected. (1) Constant Error (CE) is the length of

time that a respondent varied from the given beat when performing a synchronization exercise. Measurements were recorded as positive if the respondent was late, and negative if he/she was early. (2) Absolute Error (AE), therefore, is the absolute value of the CE measurements. This measurement is necessary because the negative and positive values cancel each other out in the data collection process. (3) Variability Error (VE) is the standard deviation or consistency in the performance of the respondents.

The data were presented as a comparison between the results of the first test and the second. The authors state that future research will develop norms to which these scores can be compared, which would certainly make the data more useful and relevant. However, the data as presented shows only small changes in the percentage of AE between the first and second tests.

The author concluded that the RPT-R may be useful for diagnosing a student's rhythmic aptitude or a student's ability to play in synchronicity with an ensemble, and to determine the progress a student makes while being instructed in rhythmic performance.

Conclusions

Considering the availability of technology as a part of today's educational community, it is important that we ask ourselves how we can use that technology to enhance the experiences we provide our students. All 5 of the studies examined herein conclude that technology integration into the music education environment provides a positive change. These authors agree that students learn as efficiently as do students in a more traditional environment, students view the use of technology with a positive attitude, and they enjoy learning using it.

We must, however, take a careful look at the drawbacks to the uses of technology that were tested in these 5 experiments. In one case, students chose to avoid challenging themselves. Rather, they viewed the technological integration as game-like. Some of the uses of technology proved to become less effective over time, while a lack of retention of information was a problem in another case.

Certainly, as suggested by the authors, more research is needed in this area to help music teachers use technology as a tool. Dawson (1995) states, "The way music was taught 20 years ago will not work with today's students. Technology is a part of nearly every discipline. It is not a fad and it is not going to go away." It may help us teach more effectively and our students learn more efficiently.

References

Bush, J. (2000) The Effects of a Hypermedia Program, Cognitive Style, and Gender on Middle School Students' Music Achievement. *Contributions to Music Education.* 27(1), 9–26.

Dawson, B. (1995) An Introductory Course in Music Technology for High School and College Level. Proceedings of Technological Directions in Music Learning. Retrieved October 17, 2000, from the World Wide Web: http://music.utsa.edu/tdml/.

Meeuwsen, H., Flohr, J. & Fink, R. (2000) Computerized Assessment of Synchronization and the Imitation and Timing of Rhythm Patterns. Proceedings of Technological Directions in Music Learning. Retrieved August 25, 2000, from the World Wide Web: http://music.utsa.edu/tdml/.

Orman, E. (1998) Effect of Interactive Multimedia Computing on Young Saxophonists' Achievement and Attitude. *Journal of Research in Music Education.* 46(1), 62–74.

Repp, R. (1999) The Feasibility of Technology Saturation for Intermediate Students of Applied Voice. Proceedings of Technological Directions in Music Learning. Retrieved August 25, 2000, from the World Wide Web: http://music.utsa.edu/tdml/

Simms, B. (1998) The Effect of an Educational Computer Game on Motivation to Learn Basic Music Skills: A Qualitative Study. Proceedings of Technological Directions in Music Learning. Retrieved August 25, 2000, from the World Wide Web: http://music.utsa.edu/tdml/.

This article first appeared in the March 2001 issue of the Florida Music Educator. *Reprinted by permission.*

Efficiency and Transformation: The Impact of Technology on Music Education. A response to Carlesta Spearman's article "How will societal and technological changes affect the teaching of music?" Vision 2020: The Housewright Symposium on the future of music education

Maud Hickey

In her *Vision 2020* chapter, Carlesta Spearman accomplishes the exceptional task of providing readers with answers to questions about how societal and technological changes will affect music teaching in the future. She begins by providing us with statistics about looming societal changes and then reminds us that technology is one of those changes. Societal and technological changes are advancing at a pace too fast for us to sensibly comprehend even the immediate, much less future implications.

Although Spearman acknowledges that the "computer has become central to our way of life," she points out the potential problems this causes, such as personal isolation, greater stratification of the "haves and have nots," and inequity in education. Trends on the horizon that Spearman predicts include more growth in computer-assisted instruction (CAI) for music teaching and learning, the development of new cultur-

Find the complete text of Carlesta Spearman's article at www.menc.org/publication/vision2020/spearman.html.

al symbols created via computer animation, and a growth of technology in such abundance and complexity that it will create a growing sense "that music surrounds us and is simply a part of life." (2000, p. 161). Her point that "quantity is not synonymous with high quality" (p. 161) however, is an important, yet often overlooked warning. Spearman then offers a list of positive developments that technology will or has already brought to music teaching: direct commerce from composers and performers to consumers; more creative and animated teaching tools; distance education; interactive, computer-based instruction; music accompaniment programs; cyberspace communication and dissemination of information; and less gender stratification. Spearman also recognizes that CAI will offer programs that "stimulate music experiences associated with composition and improvisation" (p. 161).

In this essay, I will expand upon two points that Spearman briefly mentions: one point pertains to computer use in music composition and the other examines the related area of music literacy. In adjacent sentences Spearman refers to both: "Having the computer resources to make it possible to create original music does not mean the user will become an expert composer. Furthermore, an intelligent consumer of this musical information requires a high level of music literacy and maturity" (p. 161). I will argue that musicians as well as consumers do not necessarily need a "higher" level of music literacy—in the traditional sense—but a different *kind* of music literacy. Secondly, that this new kind of music literacy will have a profound effect on ways in which we approach and teach music composition and music in general. And finally, I will discuss the fact that using the computer, as Spearman says, will not necessarily make one an "expert" composer, but certainly a different kind of composer than previously imagined.

The Transformative Power of Technology

In an intriguing article about how music teaching will be affected by technology, David Beckstead (2001) posits two possibilities for the use of technology in music teaching and learning: as a tool of efficiency and as a tool of transformation.[1] The conveniences of downloading music from the Internet, of having direct commerce opportunities for composers and performers, and the ability to use music technology to enhance and even quicken knowledge gained in music history, theory, reading, ear training, etc. are examples of some of the ways in which technology has fostered greater efficiency in music teaching and learning. Even music composition, in the traditional sense, can be taught more quickly than before because of the notation and sequencing tools that are available—instant input, recording, and notation, along with capability to edit and hear one's editions instantly provide methods for music composition that are more efficient than ever. In the past, while children were certainly able to compose using traditional acoustical instruments, and even hear these immediately via tape-recorded feedback, the instantaneous nature of feedback and the availability of a much wider and richer palette of available musical sounds that new technologies provide opens the world of music composition to children in more novel ways. For this reason alone, teachers should take advantage of music technology for teaching composition to children. However, in order to understand the real transformative power of technology in music education we need only to look at the ways in which technology has already changed music making and how technological tools offer qualitatively different methods for music composition and music learning.

Seymour Papert was one of the first to aggressively tout the transformative power of computers in education. In the classic book, *Mindstorms* (1980), Papert describes the program LOGO that he created which allows children a qualitatively deeper and more meaningful understanding of mathematics. In describing the power of LOGO and the computer, Papert asserts:

The child, even at preschool ages, is in control: The child programs the computer. And in teaching the computer how to think, children embark on an exploration about how they themselves think. The experience can be heady: Thinking about thinking turns the child into an epistemologist, an experience not even shared by most adults. (p. 19)

Papert urged educators to think of computer technology as a powerful means for teaching children not only to "know about" a phenomenon, but to better "know how." As Papert identified the computer's power in mathematics education, I would extend the supposition that it can also profoundly change techniques toward and access to music composition, and therefore music teaching and learning. An analogy is to compare the impact that the phonograph had on music listening and music appreciation to the impact computers will have on music learning and music composition. While the phonograph allowed music listeners for the first time to hear music from places and people beyond what they or somebody in the same room performed, computer music technology allows people, for the first time, to compose for mediums other than human performers. Computer technology has also provided new approaches and techniques for music composition. Most importantly, the new computer technology can provide qualitatively different and more meaningful access to music composition for children than previously available, and therefore should positively affect music learning.

A New Music Literacy

In music education, the transformative nature of technology has created a new kind of "literacy" and has created access to music composition previously barricaded by notational knowledge. Papert coined the terms "letteracy" and "letterate" to mean the traditional way we refer to the state of being able to read and write. He defines the terms literacy and literate to mean more holistic "ways of knowing" in a domain (1993, p. 10). Computer technology, says Papert:

… breaks down the barriers that traditionally separate the preletterate from the letterate, the concrete from the abstract, the bodily from the disembodied. By straddling these divisions it removes an obstacle that has kept many people from crossing from the concrete, body-syntonic orality of childhood to forms of competence that have in the past been accessible only in literate, abstract, and decorporalized forms. (1993, p. 49).

Using Papert's terminology, letteracy in music pertains to one's ability to read and write standard music notation. Music literacy refers to a more comprehensive "knowing" of music. Computer technology has clearly helped to eliminate the barrier of standardized notation for those not yet "letterate" by providing tools that allow one to manipulate and create music and notate music without prerequisite understanding of abstract notation. Technology has also created a new kind of music "literacy" and aesthetic as it provides infinite possibilities of new synthesized sounds as well as software that allows free manipulation of these new sounds (as well as traditional sounds) in completely new ways and by those who, in the past, did not have access. Because of technology, music composition has changed drastically in two ways: Composers can now create for mediums beyond human performance limitations, and music composition (and I will argue, music listening and learning) can now be approached in a less elemental and more holistic manner.

A New Music Composition

Edgar Varese is noted as a pioneer by composing for machines (such as the tape recorder) to perform in compositions (e.g., *Deserts* for wind, percussion, and tape, 1954, and *Poème électronique,* 1958). Paul Lansky's recording *Idle Chatter* (1985) is an excellent example of the use of human voices as the "instrument," but it being manipulated electronically to the point that the voices are no longer recognizable as human voices. The compositions cannot be performed live by human voices, only by the computer.

Besides the "computer as performer" and its accessibility of new synthesized sounds, computer technology has also produced new possibilities for music composition techniques. One striking example of a new composition technology is the growing influx of "mixing" software that emulates approaches to music making by DJs and hip-hop artists. Software such as EZMixer, Mixman, and Virtual DeeJay provide the user (composer) with tools to mix digital music files and add layers of pulsating rhythmic tracks and "bass tracks" to create completely new compositions. "Remix" composition technology amasses a collaborative effort between several composers, with the creative effort at the end by the artist who makes the new "mixture" and layers it with new rhythms. This new approach to composition is described in the manual for the software Mixman:

> In recent years there has been a significant amount of hype about electronic music, remixes and DJ

culture. Record companies have always remixed versions of songs to breathe new life into them or make them appeal to a specific music market. A slow ballad might be turned into a stylish dance song. But what is a remix? A remix in its truest sense is the art of taking elements from an existing song and adding new musical elements in order to augment or change the feel of the original song. It is quite common today to find artists that alter the original parts of a song to the point at which the line between remixing and composing is significantly blurred. As we approach the new millennium, with software like Mixman Studio, the definition of DJ, artist, remixer and producer will continue to change and grow. (p. 3–2).

In a remarkably simple way, technology's effect on the changing nature of music composition becomes most apparent when observing children compose music using computers. Using simple music sequencing software connected to synthesizer keyboards, one can now compose by copying, cutting, moving, and pasting (several times!) large blocks of sounds. Instant "arrangements" can be created by moving and copying and deleting and repeating and layering several sections previously saved and then put into final order in post hoc fashion. Imagine a child beginning her composition by first recording a broad sweep of sounds produced by a long glissando motion over the synthesizer keyboard. Then she copies and pastes this musical gesture, several times staggered, each time with a different "patch"[2] over a 15–second time span to result in a sweeping, wave-like sound for the introduction to her music. She saves this and at the conclusion of her music, pastes it into the composition, unrecognizable, however, because she augments and transposes the gesture as it fades out to end the piece. Or a child creates an interesting dance-like "gesture" that he then copies and pastes every other 10 seconds or so, either in a track underneath another musical idea or pasted by itself, but with a new "patch" to create a perfect rondo form composition. The terms "gesture," "seconds," "patch," and "track" have replaced the traditional terms melodic, measures, instrument and voice. (With "pitch bend" features on hardware and tone-bend manipulation in software, melodic possibilities also include semi-tones). This more "holistic" approach to music composition would be virtually impossible without music technology.

In a very drastic sense, computer technology may move us away from starting with the traditional emphasis in composition, for example, on the ability and skill to craft a fine melody, toward the skills of creating and moving and manipulating larger musical gestures.[3] This would no doubt affect the approach to teaching music. If children's "way of knowing" music through computer technology is enabled through creating and manipulating music in the ways described, then teaching the staid elemental concepts of melody separate from rhythm and harmony (for example) begins to feel artificial. Rob Cutietta's suggestion that the musical elements are not the best tools for teaching music (1993) seems especially pertinent in light of new music composition technology. Cutietta proposed five "perceptual elements" instead of the musical elements as an alternative approach to music teaching. The elements motion, energy, flow, fabric, and color are more closely related to ways in which children now approach music composition with technology.

Computer Technology and Music Research

Researchers have used computer technology to observe children's manipulation of musical sounds. Long before the arrival of common computer composition software, Jeanne Bamberger observed children as they manipulated "tune blocks" on a screen in order to better understand their perceptual approach and comprehension of music (1972, 1974, 1977). Bamberger recently created CAI software using the same philosophy. It is called Impromptu and accompanies a musical appreciation book titled *Developing Musical Intuitions* (Bamberger, 2000). In the program, users move tune blocks on the screen to create new songs or recreate the "right song." Her reasons for this approach to research and CAI software resonate with the philosophy of Seymour Papert: "The games and exercises provided by the Impromptu software are nothing more or less than exercises in self-knowledge: through manipulating basic musical objects, one discovers what one already knows, and one builds on that" (2000, p. x).

Folkestad, Lindstrom, and Hargreaves (1997) found evidence of two kinds of compositional strategies used by children as they composed using computer technology: horizontal and vertical. The "horizontal" composers completed their compositions in form and content from beginning to end (i.e., used the computer as a "tape recorder"). These composers often had good keyboard skills and wrote traditional melody with harmony types of compositions (rhythm was secondary). A second kind of "horizontal" composer composed on an acoustic instrument first, then recorded the finished ideas onto the computer track by track. The com-

puter was seen as a "co-musician" in those cases.

The "vertical" composers displayed an approach to composition discussed earlier; that is, composition not possible *without* computer technology. Compositions were recorded "chunk by chunk" with frequent back tracking to rerecord ideas and that showed no a priori notion of the whole. The types of compositions were nontraditional (i.e., melody with accompaniment) and more "soundscape"-like. "Composition and arrangement/instrumentation are conceived as one integrated process" (1997, p. 5). In this sense the computer was used as an interactive medium to a greater extent than in horizontal composition.

Folkestad, Lindstrom, and Hargreaves (1997) have provided the first glimpse of research evidence to confirm that music composition using technology provides a completely new approach to composition by children. There is much to learn yet about the impact of technology on music composition, as well music teaching and learning, and research in these areas is needed.

Conclusion

Music "letteracy," music "literacy," music composition, and music learning have been transformed because of computer technology. Beyond making it merely easier to produce music, the computer is a creative tool that opens the door for new processes and new kinds of music. The computer offers both efficient and transformative creative opportunities for music teaching and learning. That children can use computer technology to manipulate and create music in such powerful ways underscores its significant transformative power. Hopefully teachers are able to embrace this power to enhance the musical experiences of children.

Footnotes

1. Beckstead credits Sara Kiesler for the dichotomous idea of transformation versus efficiency (Kiesler uses "amplify" rather than efficiency): Kiesler, S. (1992). Talking, teaching, and learning in network groups. In A. Kaye, ed., *Collaborative learning through computer conferencing*, (147–165) Berlin: Springer-Verlag.

2. Patch in music software terms refers to the instrument choice.

3. It is not being suggested that the ability to compose a fine melody will be abandoned; only that its emphasis may be lessened or come later in the composition teaching method.

References

Bamberger, J. (1972). *Developing a musical ear: a new experiment.* (Artificial Intelligence Memo No. 264). Cambridge, MA: Massachusetts Institute of Technology, Artificial Intelligence Lab. (ERIC Document Reproduction Service No. ED 118 364).

Bamberger J. (1974). *The luxury of necessity.* (Logo memo No. 12). Cambridge, MA: Massachusetts Institute of Technology, Artificial Intelligence Lab. (ERIC Document Reproduction Service No. ED 115 535).

Bamberger, J. (1977). In search of a tune. In D. Perkins and B. Leondar (Eds.), *The arts and cognition* (pp. 284–319). Baltimore: Johns Hopkins University Press.

Bamberger, J. (2000). *Developing musical intuitions: A project-based introduction to making and understanding music.* NY: Oxford University Press.

Beckstead, D. (2001). Will technology transform music education? *Music Educators Journal,* 87(6), 44–49.

Cutietta, R. (1993). The musical elements. Who said they were right? *Music Educators Journal,* 79 (9), 48–53.

Folkestad, G., Lindstrom, B., and Hargreaves, D. J. (1997). Young people's music in the digital age. *Research Studies in Music Education,* 9, 1–12.

Papert, S. (1993). *The children's machine. Rethinking school in the age of the computer.* NY: Basic Books.

Papert, S. (1980). *Mindstorms: Children, computers, and powerful ideas.* NY: Basic Books.

Spearman, C. E. (2000). How will societal and technological changes affect the teaching of music? In C. K. Madsen (ed.) *Vision 2020: The Housewright symposium on the future of music education,* pp. 155–184. Reston, VA: MENC.

This article first appeared in the Spring 2002 issue of the Illinois Music Educator. *Reprinted by permission.*

Digital Technologies in the Music Classroom
Peter McCoy

Recently, controversy surrounding the use of digital technology in the classroom has begun to crystallize. In a February 24, 1999, column entitled "School Matters," then State Superintendent John Silber wrote that computers are "complicated and seductive typewriters with television screens attached to them" that threaten to inhibit students' abilities to learn to read and write. Privately, some well-known Massachusetts music educators have also raised questions about the role of computers in the classroom. Before we choose sides and cry "Luddite" or rush off to join the flat-earth society, however, music educators should consider what digital technologies such as the computer enable students to do musically. Can students using computers do musical things better or faster than before, or even do things that they could not do before?

The answers to these questions hinge upon the many ways in which digital technologies are changing music teaching and learning in the schools. Fundamentally, we must address the questions, "How might new roles for digital technologies change the ways in which students learn and, concomitantly, how teachers teach and assess student learning?" The term "digital technology" is used here in place of the more traditional term "computer" because the use of digital technologies and digital media has expanded to encompass nearly every aspect of modern life. As the line between the familiar box-on-a-desk and other electronic devices dissolves, teachers and students may find a wide new array of tools at their disposal. Recent examples include the popular MP3 format and Internet services provided via cellular telephone. These technologies (as well as others as yet unimagined) mean that the delivery of musical content is becoming decentered, both spatially and temporally.

How might new roles for digital technology change the ways in which students learn?
Imagine, for example, a classroom filled with elementary students sharing the results of a world-wide listening treasure hunt they have completed using personal devices no larger than a pager. Imagine a rehearsal in which an orchestra conductor says to her brass section, "Let's go for more of a Reiner/CSO sound at letter G," and the students are able to call up, listen to, and compare multiple CD-quality examples of the excerpt in question "on the spot." Imagine a student in a voice lesson able to research differences in singing practice between the French Baroque and the Italian Renaissance so easily that the flow of the lesson is not disrupted. Such possibilities are just around the corner.

Today, digital technologies are being used by students as both a content resource and a process tool. CD-ROM and Web-based resources now provide vast interdisciplinary opportunities, fostering historical and multicultural understandings of music as a human activity and music among the arts. Sequencing software allows students a richer and more flexible environment in which to sing, play, improvise, compose, and arrange music. Most importantly, notation and sequencing software afford students the opportunity to do something they have never been able to do before: capture, edit, arrange, and share their musical ideas with peers, teachers, parents, and the local and global community. The music education profession is only beginning to recognize the cognitive developmental implications of this new opportunity to capture, edit, and share emerging musical thoughts.

How might new roles for digital technology change the ways in which we teach?

Teachers may more easily become partners in a "community of learners" due to an expanding range of possible learning outcomes. Teachers may become process guides rather than comprehensive content resources; no single teacher could begin to memorize the wealth of information contained in CD-ROM and Internet-based resources, nor should they. These content resources provide teachers with access to almost unlimited information about musical instruments, ensembles, styles, genres, cultures, and trends, etc. Scope of inquiry may be expanded due to removal of side-based resource limitations, or the scope of inquiry may be delimited due to ability to conduct refined Boolean searches of these vast information sources. Students will more easily be able to apply knowledge rather than simply work to collect factual information and skills. For example, students can now demonstrate the evolution of their understanding of performance practice, arrange a MIDI file, transform a digitized sound file, or create a multimedia presentation. Such demonstrations allow students to "show what they know" in ways previously unavailable to them. Teachers and students can more easily collaborate over great distances by sharing multimedia over the Internet. In addition to providing students and teachers access to expert consultants, this distance learning may lead to expanded opportunities for team-teaching and collaboration between students and teachers in remote locations.

How might these new roles for digital technology change the ways in which we assess?

Student activity is more likely to be project centered, and will generate products that may be collected into formative or summative portfolios. Portfolios may be reviewed by teachers, peers, students, parents, and the community. Checklists of concepts and skills may be used to document the evolution of the portfolio; annotations that accompany each piece within the portfolio could describe the objective achieved and the related content standard. Portfolios may be managed with site-based software or they may be Internet-based. A CD-ROM containing the personal portfolio could be issued to each child, facilitating documentation across grade, building, or district changes. Digital portfolios will become indispensable in an increasingly mobile society.

Can students using digital technologies do musical things better or faster than before or do things that they could not do before?

Clearly, digital technologies represent a powerful new set of tools for the music educator—tools that are already facilitating the implementation of the National Standards in schools across the country. Students today have access to content and facilitated processes that were simply unavailable to their parents. Whether this access and attendant change is for good or ill will depend entirely upon how these tools are used. Music educators have always been quick to take advantage of new developments in sound production and reproduction to enhance music learning and assessment. With thoughtful application, emerging digital technologies represent a dramatic expansion of opportunity to engage in musical thinking.

How might new roles for digital technology change the ways in which we educate future music teachers?

Digital technology must be integrated into the teacher-education process. This means that courses throughout collegiate and continuing music education curricula must engage preservice and inservice teachers in activities that involve the use of digital technologies. Since teachers tend to reproduce their own learning experiences in the classroom, it will be important that those experiences demonstrate their musical growth.

Can interacting with digital technology in a musical context improve the nature of students' musical thinking?

Digital technologies are not a panacea for the music classroom; they are only useful to the extent that they allow students and teachers to function in ways that are faster or easier than before or to do things they could not do before. We don't yet know whether creative use of digital technologies will result in a more musical or better musically-educated society; only time and careful study may tell. Modern digital technologies will not replace traditional ways of being musical—singing, playing, moving, listening—because these traditional modalities involve combinations of intelligences that have stood the test of time. The kinesthetic processes of singing and playing acoustic instruments will continue to have appeal for future generations as for past. Rather, digital technologies will take their place beside these more traditional ways of being musical. The emerging potential of digital technologies to support, expand, and transform musical thought will continue to change the way in which musicianship develops and, by extension, the ways in which it is cultivated in the modern music classroom.

This article originally appeared in the Fall 2000 issue of the Massachusetts Music News. *Reprinted by permission.*

Digitization and Diversity
Roseanne Rosenthal

It would be hard to miss the fact that computer technology is changing society and the nature of education. In higher education, new technology and diversity standards are in place that must be demonstrated by teacher education institutions,[1] and by the students who are graduating from their programs. If all goes as planned, Illinois-trained teachers will be entering their first jobs with a comfortable working knowledge of computer technology and how it may be used in their work as educators. Similarly, every institution in the state is (or soon will be) working to develop coursework, experiences, and an overall educational environment that equitably and sufficiently prepares the new graduate for a more diverse society. They will need the tools that will help them do everything in their power to assure that any division between the "haves" and "have nots," and between the many cultures that are shaping our society, is weakened, not enhanced, through the use of technology and music.

Three years ago, Carlesta Spearman wrote the article appearing in this journal titled "How Will Societal and Technological Changes Affect Society." She envisioned the potential of technology in 2020 to change music education. She also argued that technology provides a way for educators to adapt to the demographic shifts occurring in this country. She probably did not anticipate that much of her thinking would become commonplace by 2002.

Technology is here. A more diverse society is here. Those who attended this past January's IMEA conference and heeded the array of technological offerings could not fail to be impressed with the potential and possibilities inherent in the technology sessions and on the exhibit floor. One also could not fail to observe a heightened sensitivity to the diversity of our society evident in numerous sessions.

Spearman does, however, indirectly raise some philosophical concerns about the role of technology and societal changes in music education. Is technology restructuring interests in music? Is technology changing the things we think about in music? Are the symbols and sounds we use to think with when we think about music changing? Is the community of people who are thinking about music actually changing? And, related to this, what is the role of higher education in the process?

A very recent article entitled "Where Music Will Be Coming From"[2] suggests answers to these questions that may have repercussions for music educators. The author contends that "there is no music today that has not been shaped by the fact of recording and duplication." As a result, 3 forces appear to be shaping the future of music: (1) access to highly perfected music on CDs, (2) the fact that much music may be obtained for free via the Web, and (3) the liquidity of digitized sound. He suggests that when we perform music in this day and age we are performing for a "technological ear." If this is true, then the things we think about in music are being restructured, as is our vocabulary, and the community of people engaged in active music listening and creativity.

For example, playing for a technological ear suggests a level of performance precision that will withstand repeated listening and duplication. Technological advances in music education software and in recording technology enable the learner to perfect his or her performance to the level that a technological ear demands. Even our contemporary music festivals, where clinicians speak comments into tape recorders, serve this need.

Find the complete text of Carlesta Spearman's article at www.menc.org/publication/vision2020/spearman.html.

One ramification for music education is that the level of performance quality that is expected from the average musician is high. Anyone who fails to listen to recordings, rich or poor, and regardless of culture, is often left in the dust, disadvantaged by failing to develop the precision that a technological ear demands. It's easy to envision both bright and dark outcomes to this scenario. How we deal with this scenario may well become increasingly important in the future of music teacher education.

The second point of the article referred to above is that digitization has made duplication easy: "Copies are so ubiquitous, so cheap (free, in fact) that the only things truly valuable are *those which cannot be copied.*" When this happens, what becomes valuable, of course, is what cannot be duplicated. Music educators' abilities to organize methods to navigate the approximately 30,000 new releases or rereleases of music offered each year, direct attention to worthwhile Web sites, create playlists, or catalog listening examples may become increasingly valued assets in the near future.

Other attributes that cannot be duplicated, and which music teachers bring to their programs, are kindness, honesty, sincerity, trustworthiness, hopefulness, appreciation of the uniqueness of each student's humanity, and a sense of the preciousness of the human condition under all circumstances, but especially in live music, ideally performed by a diverse group of children. Maybe we will need to do a better job of cultivating these traits in our future teachers.

The third new power that is resulting from technology is the liquidity and fluidity of digitally produced music. Kelly puts it this way:

> Once music is digitized, new behaviors emerge. With liquid music you have the power to reorder the sequence of tunes on an album, or among albums. To surgically morph a sound until it is suitable for new use. To precisely extract from someone else's music a sample of notes to use oneself. To X-ray the guts of music and outline its structure, and then alter it. To substitute new lyrics. To rearrange a piece so that its parts yield a different voice. To re-engineer a piece so that it sounds better on a car woofer. To meld and marry music together into hybrid breeds. To shorten a piece, or to draw it out so that it takes twice as long to play.

Contemporary designers of music education software, users of digitization technology, and teens who download, swap, and build CDs acquired from the Internet or from recording booths at concerts take the liquidity of digitized music for granted. It seems inevitable that dealing with music's liquidity will play a greater and greater role in music education. If so, our teachers will need to be prepared to be leaders in the processes involved in digital manipulation of sound.

The effects of technology on music, education, and society's diversity still remain to be seen. With all due respect to Spearman's ideas, it may, however, be the middle-class child who is reaping the least benefit of the new power of music technology. Among some of the more diverse ethnic communities, deconstructing and reconstructing music is a recreational activity. It just is not necessarily mainstream music that is being used. Similarly, in schools with ample technological budgets and a creative vision of music education, students have the opportunity to work with musician-teachers who are well aware of technology's creative promise. Perhaps the well-programmed middle American child is most at-risk for being left behind in creative experimentation with the power of technology to help perfect, duplicate, and manipulate sound in music.

In conclusion, the concerns Spearman describes in her article appear to have advanced and morphed considerably since the publication of *Vision 2020*. Higher education bears a tremendous responsibility, one that is not lost on the Illinois State Board of Education and many members of our own music education community, to assure that educators are adept at incorporating technology and human diversity into their teaching. Our greatest opportunity and responsibility may be to figure out what to teach to the new generation of children who are growing up with digitized technology. We may even be on the threshold of an era of musical inventiveness that is so comfortable with including all people in the musical experience that it is simply taken for granted. If so, then music educators at all levels will continue, like always, to teach far more than just music through music. Technology will probably not change this power of music.

Footnotes

1. Teacher preparation institutions must demonstrate that their graduates possess knowledge and performance skills in nine areas, as follows:

Standard 1: Basic Computer Technology Operations and Concepts

Standard 2: Personal and Professional Uses of Technology

Standard 3: Application of Technology in Instruction

Standard 4: Social, Ethical, and Human Issues

Standard 5: Productivity Tools

Standard 6: Telecommunications and Information Access

Standard 7: Research, Problem Solving, and Product Development

Standard 8: Information Literacy Skills

Standard 9: Collaborative Planning and Teaching

2. Kevin Kelly. "Where Music Will Be Coming From." *The New York Times Magazine,* March 17, 2002.

This article first appeared in the Spring 2002 issue of the Illinois Music Educator. *Reprinted by permission.*

A Philosophy and Strategies for Technology in Music Education
Karl D. Swearingen

Computer technology is all around us and has literally become a part of our day-to-day existence as educators, musicians, and consumers. Even the ownership of personal computers is approaching that of the television. According to recent media polls, 67% of all households in the United States now own some form of computer and use the Internet on a regular basis for e-mail, surfing, and consumerism. Our students now come to our music rooms with expectations of technology inclusion and curriculum, which is prevalent and growing in other subjects. These students now have a tremendous literacy and facility in technology and have a keen interest in the integration of such technology in their lives.

As we begin our new school year and attend the preterm meetings, primary district status messages from administrators will primarily include technology usage, federal and state mandates for technology, upgrade priorities, status of technology in the classrooms, and, of course, money. It seems that when we discuss and submit the capital outlay budgets in our respective school sites with our administrators, the necessity and monetary urgency for a tuba, piano, or choral risers seems to get placed on the "pile." But when we express a need for computers, there is a definite difference in response; usually a response with more fervor and often a "yes we have the budget for that" answer. However, we may encounter the answer, "Why does music need a computer?" So there we sit, looking for the answer to that question from our administrator. Then we scramble to define, on the spot mind you, the answer and framework. This question, and the whole issue of technology in music education, is in dire need of definition of what and why. In other words, music educators must develop a philosophy of technology inclusion with appropriate usage with concurrent strategies for effective long range and future development.

A Philosophy of Technology in Music Education

In developing this philosophy, we must first define technology's role in music. This is important, as we need to put technology in a role that is compatible with the acoustic tradition of music and also in a role that does not create another "fad" that collects dust.

We can define technology in music education two ways:

1. A supportive role that enhances the current, traditional acoustic curriculum, and
2. A "portal" for music for all students.

In both cases we are thinking about a philosophy that gives the student(s) the opportunity to make music and to be engaged in "musicing" (Elliot, 1995), which is why they are there to begin with.

Let us first examine the "supportive role," which is the most common method in which technology is utilized in the secondary and higher education levels, and where the basis for music learning tends to be performance-based. Here we are concerned with a philosophy that essentially "attaches" technology to extend curriculum. Philosophically we are thinking about:

• Music fundamentals
• Theory
• History
• Creativity and improvisation
• Research via the Internet on music and cross-curricular subjects
• Writing

By examining and critically thinking about these 6 areas, we have addressed and included the National Standards, state frameworks, and the basic skills in which each district wants our students to have competency and literacy. At the same time we broaden our students' knowledge and literacy in the subject of music.

The second philosophical aspect is that which defines technology in music education as a "portal to music for all students." The concept is that technology affords another doorway to music for any and all students, whether they play an instrument or sing or have no previous performance experience

in music at all. This portal concept is highly applicable to ages K–adult as the hardware and software now available have been developed to fully address the broadest age spectrum in music education. Also, this "portal to music for all students" gives each student the ability to make music and to be engaged in a creative process with a tangible outcome or product in the following ways:
- Creativity and improvisation
- Performance
- Consumerism and audience development in music
- Research via the Internet on music and cross-curricular subjects
- Writing.

The aforementioned points give all students the opportunity to create and become engaged in composition and especially affords a performance outlet which can be more comfortable and "user-friendly" to some students at first. But this portal philosophy can also bring students on the acoustic pathway of music by giving them the exposure and ability to be engaged in music making while fostering a desire to explore acoustical music in the form of singing or playing an instrument.

With regard to consumerism and audience development in music, when a person is engaged in the doing of music, they naturally will seek further involvement as listeners and consumers to further their interest and knowledge which has been stimulated via technology.

Therefore, in developing a philosophy of technology in music education, it is first important to understand the place that technology has and is acquiring in society. Then, look critically at how it will support music learning and provide a new portal to music for all students. Technology in music education needs a clearly defined philosophy by each music educator for effective teaching and appropriate usage with well-defined outcomes.

Strategies for Implementation of a Philosophy of Technology in Music Education

Probably the most important strategy is to define the goals, framework, usage, and instructional objectives as a music or arts department. What is key here is unity in your department to make your philosophy work and to create a useful and viable curriculum with positive outcomes. It will further be important to unify, as a team, how and with what will music technology be part of the school and your current curriculum.

Now let's take a look at some examples to illustrate these points. Last October, as part of a guest lecturer visit to Montana State University, I was afforded a visit to Bozeman High School. Their choral, band, orchestra, and academic music programs have essentially formed a technology alliance in regards to curriculum, hardware, software, and space to be used in the following manner:

In the music suite they installed Wenger practice rooms that were singles, doubled, tripled, and even quadrupled in size to accommodate general practice; utilized SmartMusic technology, introduced small-group theory instruction, composition, individual improvisation using Band-in-a Box, and researched music on the Web for academic music courses.

The Bozemen High School Music Department settled on one platform and hardware, based on district criteria and corporate partnering in the district. They chose mainstream software that is upgradeable, and applicable to all performance and nonperformance-based classes and student needs. Further, they utilized the main quad area for security, passive and active student monitoring, and multiple instructional methodologies. This is a highly successful program and a well-defined model for the senior high school level.

Last spring, at the 2001 CMEA Conference, 2 exceptional and successful programs, Hilltop High School in Chula Vista under the direction of Dennis Mauricio and Bellflower High School under the direction of Frank Perez, came to the conference to demonstrate the following:
- Successful curriculum frameworks of goals, instructional strategies, and outcomes
- Support of a traditional acoustic performance ensemble
- A new "portal to music for all students," which had them engaged in music making and composition
- Creativity and improvisation
- Research and writing
- Motivation for home practice
- New performance ensemble which is designed to prepare students to understand, handle, and have literacy with sound reinforcement, music computer technology, and recording skills.

The jazz education program at Bellflower High School has been taken to a highly successful level as evidenced at CMEA by the inclusion of improvisation software. It allows experienced and nonexperienced students to acquire improvisation skills in the rehearsal and at home by creating MIDI files of the musical assignments within an improvisation curriculum that includes performance and writing.

The Hilltop High School Tech ensemble certainly demonstrated the philosophy of the "portal to music for all students" wherein any student can become performance and musically engaged. It also provides a new performance ensemble which is designed to prepare students to understand, handle, and have literacy with sound reinforcement, music computer technology, and recording skills.

Technology is here and now in every facet of our lives. Obviously, our music curricula will be impacted. Our success with technology will not be based solely on obtaining the best equipment but how we craft the basis for technology education in music. In the 21st century, technology will be a driving force in education. Its role and success in music education will depend on a well defined philosophy, curriculum framework, and strategies.

References

Elliot, David J. (1995). *Music Matters.* New York. Oxford.

Rubin, David M. (1995). *The Desktop Musician—Creating Music With Your Computer.* Berkeley, CA. Osborne McGraw-Hill.

Rudolph, Thomas E. (1996). *Teaching Music with Technology.* Chicago, IL. GIA.

Web Sites

Bozeman High School: www.bozeman.k12.mt.us/bhsonline.

Hilltop High School Tech Ensemble: http://hhs.suhsd.k12ca.us/musictech/hhsmusictech-pages/main.htm.

This article first appeared in the Fall 2001 issue of California's CMEA Magazine. *Reprinted by permission.*

Other MENC Technology Resources

Opportunity-to-Learn Standards for Music Technology (booklet). 1999. 9 pages. #4030. To view the text of this document, visit www.menc.org.

Strategies for Teaching: Technology compiled and edited by Sam Reese, Kimberly McCord, and Kimberly Walls. 2002. 168 pages. #1657.

Participate in the
Technology Network Community
at www.menc.org.

For complete ordering information on these and other publications, contact:
MENC
Publications Sales
1806 Robert Fulton Drive
Reston, VA 20191-4348

Credit card holders may call 1-800-828-0229